AGILE PRACTICE GUIDE

Library of Congress Cataloging-in-Publication Data has been applied for.

ISBN: 978-1-62825-199-9

Published by:
Project Management Institute, Inc.
14 Campus Boulevard
Newtown Square, Pennsylvania 19073-3299 USA
Phone: +1 610-356-4600
Fax: +1 610-356-4647
Email: customercare@pmi.org
Internet: www.PMI.org

To place a Trade Order or for pricing information, please contact Independent Publishers Group:
Independent Publishers Group
Order Department
814 North Franklin Street
Chicago, IL 60610 USA
Phone: +1 800-888-4741
Fax: +1 312- 337-5985
Email: orders@ipgbook.com (For orders only)

For all other inquiries, please contact the PMI Book Service Center.
PMI Book Service Center
P.O. Box 932683, Atlanta, GA 31193-2683 USA
Phone: 1-866-276-4764 (within the U.S. or Canada) or +1-770-280-4129 (globally)
Fax: +1-770-280-4113
Email: info@bookorders.pmi.org

This Practice Guide was jointly funded by Agile Alliance® and was developed in collaboration with members of the Agile Alliance®. Agile Alliance® does not endorse any agile methodology or certification.

10 9 8 7 6 5 4 3

PREFACE

The Project Management Institute and Agile Alliance® chartered this practice guide to create a greater understanding of agile approaches in their communities. The vision for this practice guide is to equip project teams with tools, situational guidelines, and an understanding of the available agile techniques and approaches to enable better results.

Project teams are using agile approaches in a variety of industries beyond software development. Both organizations realize that expansion has created a need for a common language, open mindedness, and the willingness to be flexible in how products and deliverables are brought to market. In addition, both organizations realize there are multiple ways to achieve successful delivery. There are a broad range of tools, techniques, and frameworks; teams have choices for approaches and practices that fit their project and the organizational culture in order to achieve the desired outcome.

The *Agile Practice Guide* core committee members are from varying backgrounds and use various approaches. Some of the committee members are consultants and some work inside organizations. All have worked in agile ways for many years.

TABLE OF CONTENTS

LIST OF TABLES AND FIGURES

1

—

INTRODUCTION

Welcome to the *Agile Practice Guide*! This guide was developed as a collaborative effort by the Project Management Institute (PMI) and Agile Alliance®. The members of the core writing team who developed this practice guide included volunteers from both organizations, drawing on subject matter expertise from a broad range of current practitioners and leaders from a diverse range of backgrounds, beliefs, and cultures.

This practice guide provides practical guidance geared toward project leaders and team members adapting to an agile approach in planning and executing projects. While our core writing team recognizes there is staunch support to use predictive approaches and conversely, passion around shifting to an agile mindset, values, and principles, this practice guide covers a practical approach to project agility. This practice guide represents a bridge to understanding the pathway from a predictive approach to an agile approach. In fact, there are similar activities between the two, such as planning, that are handled differently but occur in both environments.

Our core writing team used an agile mindset to collaborate and manage the development of this first edition of the practice guide. As technology and culture changes, future updates and refinements to the practice guide will reflect current approaches.

Our core team adopted a more informal, relaxed writing style for this practice guide than is typical for PMI standards. The guide incorporates new elements, such as tips, sidebars, and case studies to better illustrate key points and concepts. Our team intends for these changes to make this practice guide more readable and user-friendly.

This practice guide goes beyond addressing the use of agile in the computer software development industry, because agile has expanded into non-software development environments. Manufacturing, education, healthcare and other industries are becoming agile to varying degrees and this use beyond software is within the scope of this practice guide.

AGILE-BASED LEARNING

Education is a prime and fertile ground to expand agile practices beyond software development. Teachers in middle schools, high schools, and universities around the world are beginning to use agile to create a culture of learning. Agile techniques are used to provide focus on prioritizing competing priorities. Face-to-face interaction, meaningful learning, self-organizing teams, and incremental and/or iterative learning that exploit the imagination are all agile principles that can change the mindset in the classroom and advance educational goals (Briggs, 2014).*

*Briggs, Sara. "Agile Based Learning: What Is It and How Can It Change Education?" *Opencolleges. edu.au* February 22, 2014, retrieved from http://www.opencolleges.edu. au/informed/features/agile-based-learning-what-is-it-and-how-can-it-change-education/

So why an *Agile Practice Guide* and why now? Project teams have used agile techniques and approaches in various forms for at least several decades. The Agile Manifesto [1][1] expressed definitive values and principles of agile as the use of agile gained substantial momentum (see Section 2.1). Today, project leaders and teams find themselves in an environment disrupted by exponential advances in technology and demands from customers for more immediate delivery of value. Agile techniques and approaches effectively manage disruptive technologies. In addition, the first principle of agile places customer satisfaction as the highest priority and is key in delivering products and services that delight customers (see Section 2.1). Rapid and transparent customer feedback loops are readily available with the widespread use of social media. Therefore, in order to stay competitive and relevant, organizations can no longer be internally focused but rather need to focus outwardly to the customer experience.

---

[1] The numbers in brackets refer to the list of references at the end of this practice guide.

Disruptive technologies are rapidly changing the playing field by decreasing the barriers to entry. More mature organizations are increasingly prone to being highly complex and potentially slow to innovate, and lag behind in delivering new solutions to their customers. These organizations find themselves competing with smaller organizations and startups that are able to rapidly produce products that fit customer needs. This speed of change will continue to drive large organizations to adopt an agile mindset in order to stay competitive and keep their existing market share.

The *Agile Practice Guide* is project-focused and addresses project life cycle selection, implementing agile, and organizational considerations for agile projects. Organizational change management (OCM) is essential for implementing or transforming practices but, since OCM is a discipline within itself, it is outside the scope of this practice guide. Those seeking guidance in OCM may refer to *Managing Change in Organizations— A Practice Guide* [2].

Additional items that are in scope and out of scope for this practice guide are listed in Table 1-1.

DISRUPTIVE TECHNOLOGY

Disruptive technology is especially enabled by the transition to cloud computing. Companies across the globe are leveraging the model for quick and cheap access to computing resources and to gain entry into traditional markets. Cloud computing requires a reduced upfront payment, but is paid over time via a subscription service, based upon a pay-as-you-go or pay-what-you-use model. Updated applications, infrastructure, and platforms are released into the cloud in an iterative and incremental fashion, keeping pace with improvements to technology and evolving customer demand.

Table 1-1. In-Scope and Out-of-Scope Items

In Scope	Out of Scope
Implementing agile approaches at a project or team level	Implementing agile throughout the organization or creating agile programs
Coverage of most popular agile approaches, as listed in industry surveys	Coverage of niche approaches, company-specific methods, or incomplete life cycle techniques
Suitability factors to consider when choosing an agile approach and/or practice	Recommending or endorsing a particular approach/practice
Mapping agile to *PMBOK® Guide* processes and Knowledge Areas	Change or modification of *PMBOK® Guide* processes and/or Knowledge Areas
Discussion on the use of agile beyond software development	Removal of software industry influence on agile approaches. (Note that software is included in this practice guide even though the use of agile is growing in many other industries beyond software.)
Guidance, techniques, and approaches to consider when implementing agile in projects or organizations	Prescriptive step-by-step instructions on how to implement agile in projects or organizations
Definitions of generally accepted terms	New terms and/or definitions

This practice guide is for project teams who find themselves in the messy middle-ground between predictive and agile approaches, who are trying to address rapid innovation and complexity, and who are dedicated to the team's improvement. This practice guide provides useful guidance for successful projects that deliver business value to meet customer expectations and needs.

This practice guide is organized as follows:

Section 2 An Introduction to Agile—This section includes the Agile Manifesto mindset, values, and principles. It also covers the concepts of definable and high-uncertainty work, and the correlation between lean, the Kanban Method, and agile approaches.

Section 3 Life Cycle Selection—This section introduces the various life cycles discussed in this practice guide. This section also addresses suitability filters, tailoring guidelines, and common combinations of approaches.

Section 4 Implementing Agile: Creating an Agile Environment—This section discusses critical factors to consider when creating an agile environment such as servant leadership and team composition.

Section 5 Implementing Agile: Delivering in an Agile Environment—This section includes information on how to organize teams and common practices teams can use for delivering value on a regular basis. It provides examples of empirical measurements for teams and for reporting status.

Section 6 Organizational Considerations for Project Agility—This section explores organizational factors that impact the use of agile approaches, such as culture, readiness, business practices, and the role of a PMO.

Section 7 A Call to Action—The call to action requests input for continuous improvement of this practice guide.

The annexes, appendixes, references, bibliography, and glossary provide additional useful information and definitions:

◆ **Annexes.** Contain mandatory information that is too lengthy for inclusion in the main body of the practice guide.

◆ **Appendixes.** Contain nonmandatory information that supplements the main body of this practice guide.

◆ **References.** Identify where to locate standards and other publications that are cited in this practice guide.

◆ **Bibliography.** Lists additional publications by section that provide detailed information on topics covered in this practice guide.

◆ **Glossary.** Presents a list of terms and their definitions that are used in this practice guide.

2

AN INTRODUCTION TO AGILE

2.1 DEFINABLE WORK VS. HIGH-UNCERTAINTY WORK

Project work ranges from definable work to high-uncertainty work. Definable work projects are characterized by clear procedures that have proved successful on similar projects in the past. The production of a car, electrical appliance, or home after the design is complete are examples of definable work. The production domain and processes involved are usually well understood and there are typically low levels of execution uncertainty and risk.

New design, problem solving, and not-done-before work is exploratory. It requires subject matter experts to collaborate and solve problems to create a solution. Examples of people encountering high-uncertainty work include software systems engineers, product designers, doctors, teachers, lawyers, and many problem-solving engineers. As more definable work is automated, project teams are undertaking more high-uncertainty work projects that require the techniques described in this practice guide.

High-uncertainty projects have high rates of change, complexity, and risk. These characteristics can present problems for traditional predictive approaches that aim to determine the bulk of the requirements upfront and control changes through a change request process. Instead, agile approaches were created to explore feasibility in short cycles and quickly adapt based on evaluation and feedback.

2.2 THE AGILE MANIFESTO AND MINDSET

Thought leaders in the software industry formalized the agile movement in 2001 with the publication of the Manifesto for Agile Software Development (see Figure 2-1).

We are uncovering better ways of developing software by doing it and helping others do it. Through this work we have come to value:

Individuals and interactions over processes and tools

Working software over comprehensive documentation

Customer collaboration over contract negotiation

Responding to change over following a plan

That is, while there is value in the items on the right, we value the items on the left more.

© 2001, the Agile Manifesto authors

Figure 2-1. The Four Values of the Agile Manifesto

Twelve clarifying principles flowed from these values as shown in Figure 2-2.

1. Our highest priority is to satisfy the customer through early and continuous delivery of valuable software.

2. Welcome changing requirements, even late in development. Agile processes harness change for the customer's competitive advantage.

3. Deliver working software frequently, from a couple of weeks to a couple of months, with a preference to the shorter timescale.

4. Business people and developers must work together daily throughout the project.

5. Build projects around motivated individuals. Give them the environment and support they need, and trust them to get the job done.

6. The most efficient and effective method of conveying information to and within a development team is face-to-face conversation.

7. Working software is the primary measure of progress.

8. Agile processes promote sustainable development. The sponsors, developers, and users should be able to maintain a constant pace indefinitely.

9. Continuous attention to technical excellence and good design enhances agility.

10. Simplicity—the art of maximizing the amount of work not done—is essential.

11. The best architectures, requirements, and designs emerge from self-organizing teams.

12. At regular intervals, the team reflects on how to become more effective, then tunes and adjusts its behavior accordingly.

Figure 2-2. The Twelve Principles Behind the Agile Manifesto

Although originating in the software industry, these principles have since spread to many other industries.

This embodiment of mindset, values, and principles defines what constitutes an agile approach. The various agile approaches in use today share common roots with the agile mindset, value, and principles. This relationship is shown in Figure 2-3.

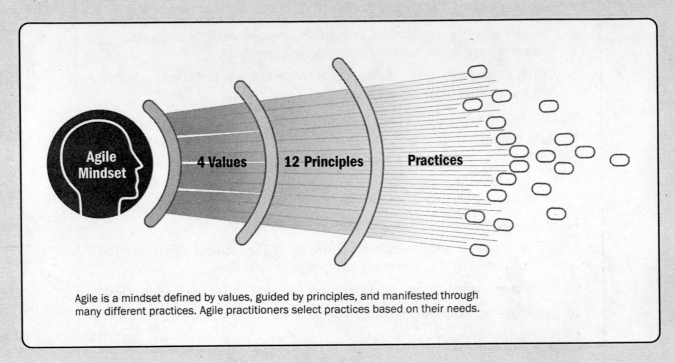

Agile is a mindset defined by values, guided by principles, and manifested through many different practices. Agile practitioners select practices based on their needs.

Figure 2-3. The Relationship Between the Agile Manifesto Values, Principles, and Common Practices

As shown in Figure 2-3, the model, inspired by Ahmed Sidky, articulates agile as a mindset defined by the Agile Manifesto values, guided by the Agile Manifesto principles, and enabled by various practices. It is worth noting that while the term "agile" became popularized after the Manifesto, the approaches and techniques being used by project teams today existed before the Agile Manifesto by many years and, in some cases, decades.

Agile approaches and *agile methods* are umbrella terms that cover a variety of frameworks and methods. Figure 2-4 places agile in context and visualizes it as a blanket term, referring to any kind of approach, technique, framework, method, or practice that fulfills the values and principles of the Agile Manifesto. Figure 2-4 also shows agile and the Kanban Method as subsets of lean. This is because they are named instances of lean thinking that share lean concepts such as: "focus on value," "small batch sizes," and "elimination of waste."

Is agile an approach, a method, a practice, a technique, or a framework? Any or all of these terms could apply depending on the situation. This practice guide, uses the term "approach" unless one of the other terms is obviously more correct.

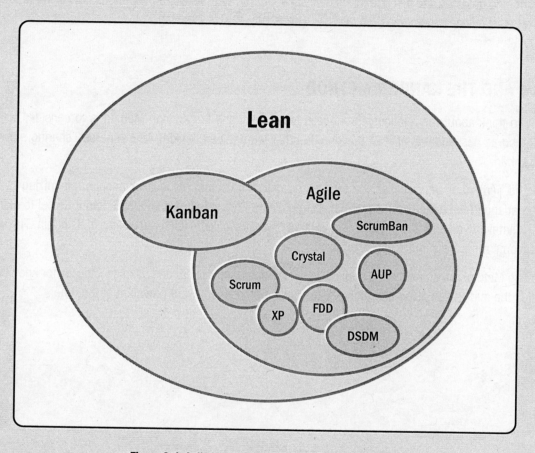

Figure 2-4. Agile is a Blanket Term for Many Approaches

In general, there are two strategies to fulfill agile values and principles. The first is to adopt a formal agile approach, intentionally designed and proven to achieve desired results. Then take time to learn and understand the agile approaches before changing or tailoring them. Premature and haphazard tailoring can minimize the effects of the approach and thus limit benefits. *(See Appendix X2 for Tailoring Considerations).*

The second strategy is to implement changes to project practices in a manner that fits the project context to achieve progress on a core value or principle. Use timeboxes to create features, or specific techniques to iteratively refine features. Consider dividing up one large project into several releases, if that works for the specific project context. Implement changes that will help the project succeed—the changes do not need to be part of the organization's formal practices. The end goal is not to be agile for its own sake, but rather to deliver a continuous flow of value to customers and achieve better business outcomes.

2.3 LEAN AND THE KANBAN METHOD

One way to think about the relationship between lean, agile, and the Kanban Method is to consider agile and the Kanban Method as descendants of lean thinking. In other words, lean thinking is a superset, sharing attributes with agile and Kanban.

This shared heritage is very similar and focuses on delivering value, respect for people, minimizing waste, being transparent, adapting to change, and continuously improving. Project teams sometimes find it useful to blend various methods—whatever works for the organization or team is what should be done regardless of its origin. The objective is the best outcome regardless of the approach used.

The Kanban Method is inspired by the original lean-manufacturing system and used specifically for knowledge work. It emerged in the mid-2000s as an alternative to the agile methods that were prevalent at the time.

The Kanban Method is less prescriptive than some agile approaches and less disruptive, as it is the original "start-where-you-are" approach. Project teams can begin applying the Kanban Method with relative ease and progress toward other agile approaches if that is what they deem necessary or appropriate. For more details on the Kanban Method, see Annex A3 on Overview of Agile and Lean Frameworks.

●●●●●

CASE

There is and probably always will be a lot of discussion around the Kanban Method and whether it belongs to the lean or agile movement. It was conceived in and around lean manufacturing, but is widely used in agile settings.

●●●●●

2.4 UNCERTAINTY, RISK, AND LIFE CYCLE SELECTION

Some projects have considerable uncertainty around project requirements and how to fulfill those requirements using current knowledge and technology. These uncertainties can contribute to high rates of change and project complexity. These characteristics are illustrated in Figure 2-5.

As project uncertainty increases, so too does the risk of rework and the need to use a different approach. To mitigate the impact of these risks, teams select life cycles that allow them to tackle projects with high amounts of uncertainty via small increments of work.

Teams can verify their work when they use small increments and can change what they do next. When teams deliver small increments, they are better able to understand the true customer requirements faster and more accurately than with a static written specification.

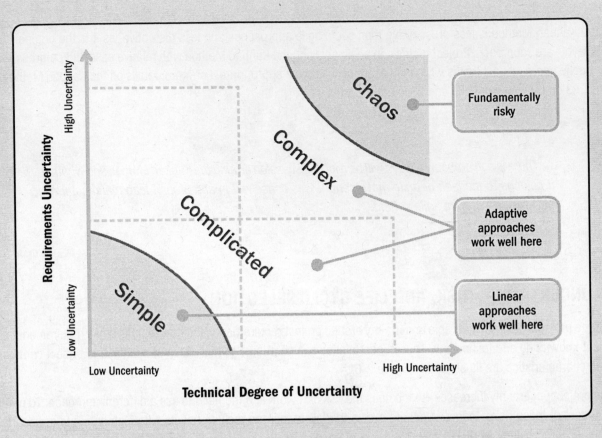

Figure 2-5. Uncertainty and Complexity Model Inspired by the Stacey Complexity Model

Teams can plan and manage projects with clear and stable requirements and clear technical challenges with little difficulty. However, as the uncertainty in the project increases, the likelihood of changes, wasted work, and rework also increases, which is costly and time consuming.

Some teams have evolved project life cycles to use iterative and incremental approaches. Many teams discover that when they explore the requirements iteratively and deliver more often incrementally, the teams adapt to changes more easily. These iterative and incremental approaches reduce waste and rework because the teams gain feedback. These approaches use:

◆ Very short feedback loops,

◆ Frequent adaptation of process,

◆ Reprioritization,

◆ Regularly updated plans, and

◆ Frequent delivery.

TIP

What do simple, complicated, and complex projects mean? Consider large projects, such as the Boston Big Dig construction project. On the surface, the project seemed fairly straightforward: move the elevated highway underground. There was high agreement on the requirements (see the Y axis in Figure 2-5). There was low uncertainty on how the project would proceed until the project started. And, as is the case for many large projects, the project encountered surprises along the way.

When a team works on a project where there is little opportunity for interim deliverables or little opportunity for prototyping, the team most likely will use a predictive life cycle to manage it. The team can adapt to what it discovers, but will not be able to use agile approaches to manage the iterative discovery of requirements or incremental deliverables for feedback.

The Big Dig project was not simple by any means. However, many projects that start out in the lower left part of the Stacey Complexity Model have no real means of moving to other approaches. Assess the project, both in the requirements and the means of delivery, to determine the best approach for the life cycle of the project.

These iterative, incremental, and agile approaches work well for projects that involve new or novel tools, techniques, materials, or application domains. (Refer to Section 3 on Life Cycle Selection). They also work well for projects that:

◆ Require research and development;

◆ Have high rates of change;

◆ Have unclear or unknown requirements, uncertainty, or risk; or

◆ Have a final goal that is hard to describe.

By building a small increment and then testing and reviewing it, the team can explore uncertainty at a low cost in a short time, reduce risk, and maximize business value delivery. This uncertainty may be centered on suitability and requirements (is the right product being built?); technical feasibility and performance (can this product be built this way?); or process and people (is this an effective way for the team to work?). All three of these characteristics—product specification, production capability, and process suitability—typically have elements of high uncertainty.

However, iterative and incremental approaches have their limits of applicability. When both technology uncertainty and requirements uncertainty are very high (the top right of Figure 2-5), the project moves beyond complex to chaotic. In order for the project to become reliably possible, it needs one of the variables (uncertainty or disagreement) to be contained.

3

LIFE CYCLE SELECTION

Projects come in many shapes and there are a variety of ways to undertake them. Project teams need awareness of the characteristics and options available to select the approach most likely to be successful for the situation.

This practice guide refers to four types of life cycles, defined as follows:

◆ **Predictive life cycle.** A more traditional approach, with the bulk of planning occurring upfront, then executing in a single pass; a sequential process.

◆ **Iterative life cycle.** An approach that allows feedback for unfinished work to improve and modify that work.

◆ **Incremental life cycle.** An approach that provides finished deliverables that the customer may be able to use immediately.

◆ **Agile life cycle.** An approach that is both iterative and incremental to refine work items and deliver frequently.

WHAT TO CALL NON-AGILE APPROACHES?

There is no single term that is universally used to describe non-agile approaches. Initially, the practice guide used the term *plan-driven* to describe the emphasis on an upfront plan and then execution of that plan. Some people prefer the terms *waterfall* or *serial* to describe this life cycle. In the end, we settled on the term *predictive* since it is used in *A Guide to the Project Management Body of Knowledge (PMBOK® Guide)* [3] and the *Software Extension to the PMBOK® Guide Fifth Edition* [4].

Many organizations do not experience either of these extremes and instead occupy some middle ground. That is natural, but we still need a way to talk about both ends of the spectrum. If *agile* is at one end, we call the other end *predictive*.

3.1 CHARACTERISTICS OF PROJECT LIFE CYCLES

Table 3-1 summarizes the characteristics of the four life cycle categories covered in this practice guide.

Table 3-1. Characteristics of Four Categories of Life Cycles

Characteristics				
Approach	**Requirements**	**Activities**	**Delivery**	**Goal**
Predictive	Fixed	Performed once for the entire project	Single delivery	Manage cost
Iterative	Dynamic	Repeated until correct	Single delivery	Correctness of solution
Incremental	Dynamic	Performed once for a given increment	Frequent smaller deliveries	Speed
Agile	Dynamic	Repeated until correct	Frequent small deliveries	Customer value via frequent deliveries and feedback

It is important to note that all projects have these characteristics—no project is completely devoid of considerations around requirements, delivery, change, and goals. A project's inherent characteristics determine which life cycle is the best fit for that project.

Another way to understand how project life cycles vary is by using a continuum ranging from predictive cycles on one end, to agile cycles on the other end, with more iterative or incremental cycles in the middle.

Figure X3-1 of Appendix X3 of the *PMBOK® Guide* – Sixth Edition displays the continuum as a flat line. This view emphasizes the shifting of project characteristics from one end to the other. Another way to visualize the continuum is with a two-dimensional square, as shown in Figure 3-1.

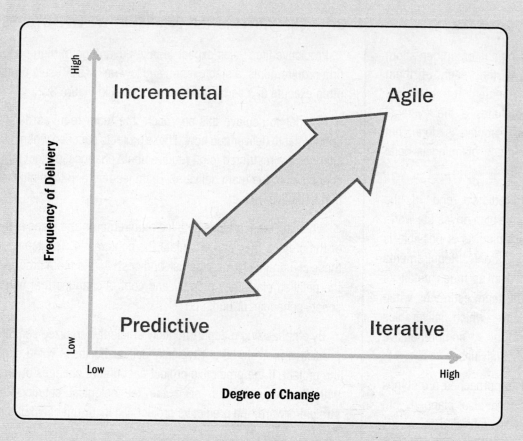

Figure 3-1. The Continuum of Life Cycles

No life cycle can be perfect for all projects. Instead, each project finds a spot on the continuum that provides an optimum balance of characteristics for its context. Specifically,

◆ **Predictive life cycles.** Take advantage of things that are known and proven. This reduced uncertainty and complexity allows teams to segment work into a sequence of predictable groupings.

◆ **Iterative life cycles.** Allow feedback on partially completed or unfinished work to improve and modify that work.

◆ **Incremental life cycles.** Provide finished deliverables that the customer may be able to use immediately.

◆ **Agile life cycles.** Leverage both the aspects of iterative and incremental characteristics. When teams use agile approaches, they iterate over the product to create finished deliverables. The team gains early feedback and provides customer visibility, confidence, and control of the product. Because the team can release earlier, the project may provide an earlier return on investment because the team delivers the highest value work first.

3.1.1 CHARACTERISTICS OF PREDICTIVE LIFE CYCLES

Predictive life cycles expect to take advantage of high certainty around firm requirements, a stable team, and low risk. As a result, project activities often execute in a serial manner, as shown in Figure 3-2.

In order to achieve this approach, the team requires detailed plans to know what to deliver and how. These projects succeed when other potential changes are restricted (e.g., requirements changes; project team members change what the team delivers). Team leaders aim to minimize change for the predictive project.

When the team creates detailed requirements and plans at the beginning of the project, they can articulate the constraints. The team can then use those constraints to manage risk and cost. As the team progresses through the detailed plan, they monitor and control changes that might affect the scope, schedule, or budget.

By emphasizing a departmentally efficient, serialized sequence of work, predictive projects do not typically deliver business value until the end of the project. If the predictive project encounters changes or disagreements with the requirements, or if the technological solution is no longer straightforward, the predictive project will incur unanticipated costs.

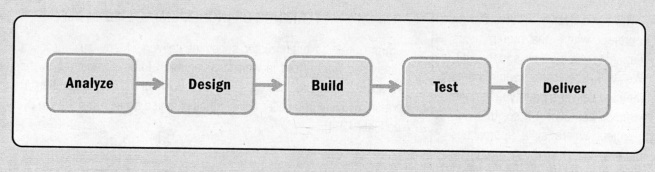

Figure 3-2. Predictive Life Cycle

3.1.2 CHARACTERISTICS OF ITERATIVE LIFE CYCLES

Iterative life cycles improve the product or result through successive prototypes or proofs of concept. Each new prototype yields new stakeholder feedback and team insights. Then, the team incorporates the new information by repeating one or more project activities in the next cycle. Teams may use timeboxing on a given iteration for a few weeks, gather insights, and then rework the activity based on those insights. In that way, iterations help identify and reduce uncertainty in the project.

Projects benefit from iterative life cycles when complexity is high, when the project incurs frequent changes, or when the scope is subject to differing stakeholders' views of the desired final product. Iterative life cycles may take longer because they are optimized for learning rather than speed of delivery.

Figure 3-3 illustrates some elements of an iterative project life cycle for a single product delivery.

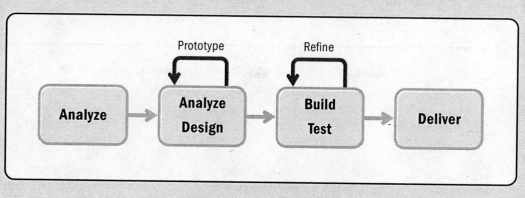

Figure 3-3. Iterative Life Cycle

Have you ever been involved on a project where the requirements seemed to change daily and thought, "We will know the requirements when we deliver a prototype that the business approves." If so, this was a project where agile approaches could have helped. A prototype encourages feedback and a better understanding of the requirements that can be incorporated into each deliverable.

3.1.3 CHARACTERISTICS OF INCREMENTAL LIFE CYCLES

Some projects optimize for speed of delivery. Many businesses and initiatives cannot afford to wait for everything to be completed; in these cases, customers are willing to receive a subset of the overall solution. This frequent delivery of smaller deliverables is called an incremental life cycle (see Figure 3-4).

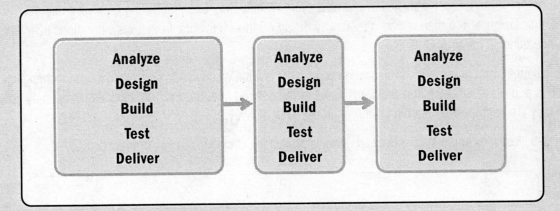

Figure 3-4. A Life Cycle of Varying-Sized Increments

TIP *Are you unsure of how a new business service might work in practice? Create a proof of concept with evaluation criteria to explore desired outcomes. Use iterative approaches when you suspect the requirements will change based on customer feedback.*

Incremental life cycles optimize work for delivering value to sponsors or customers more often than a single, final product. Teams plan initial deliverables before beginning their work, and they begin working on that first delivery as soon as possible. Some agile projects deliver value within days of project initiation. Others could take longer, ranging from 1 week to several weeks.

As the project continues, the team may deviate from the original vision. The team can manage the deviations, because the team delivers value sooner. The degree of change and variation is less important than ensuring customers get value sooner than at the end of the project.

Providing a customer a single feature or a finished piece of work is an example of the incremental approach.

For example, builders may want to show a finished room or floor of a building before they continue with the remainder of the building. In that case, they may complete a floor with fixtures, paint, and everything else intended for the finished floor before proceeding to the next floor. The customer is able to see and approve of the style, color, and other details, allowing adjustments to be made before further investments of time and money are made. This reduces potential rework and/or customer dissatisfaction.

Completeness and delivery are subjective. The team may need feedback on a prototype and may then choose to deliver a minimum viable product (MVP) to a subset of customers. The customers' feedback helps the team to learn what they need to provide for subsequent delivery of the final finished feature.

Agile teams, as a key differentiator, deliver business value often. As the product adds a broader set of features and a broader range of consumers, we say it is delivered incrementally.

3.1.4 CHARACTERISTICS OF AGILE LIFE CYCLES

In an agile environment, the team expects requirements to change. The iterative and incremental approaches provide feedback to better plan the next part of the project. However, in agile projects, incremental delivery uncovers hidden or misunderstood requirements. Figure 3-5 illustrates two possible ways to achieve incremental delivery so the project aligns with customer needs and can be adapted as necessary.

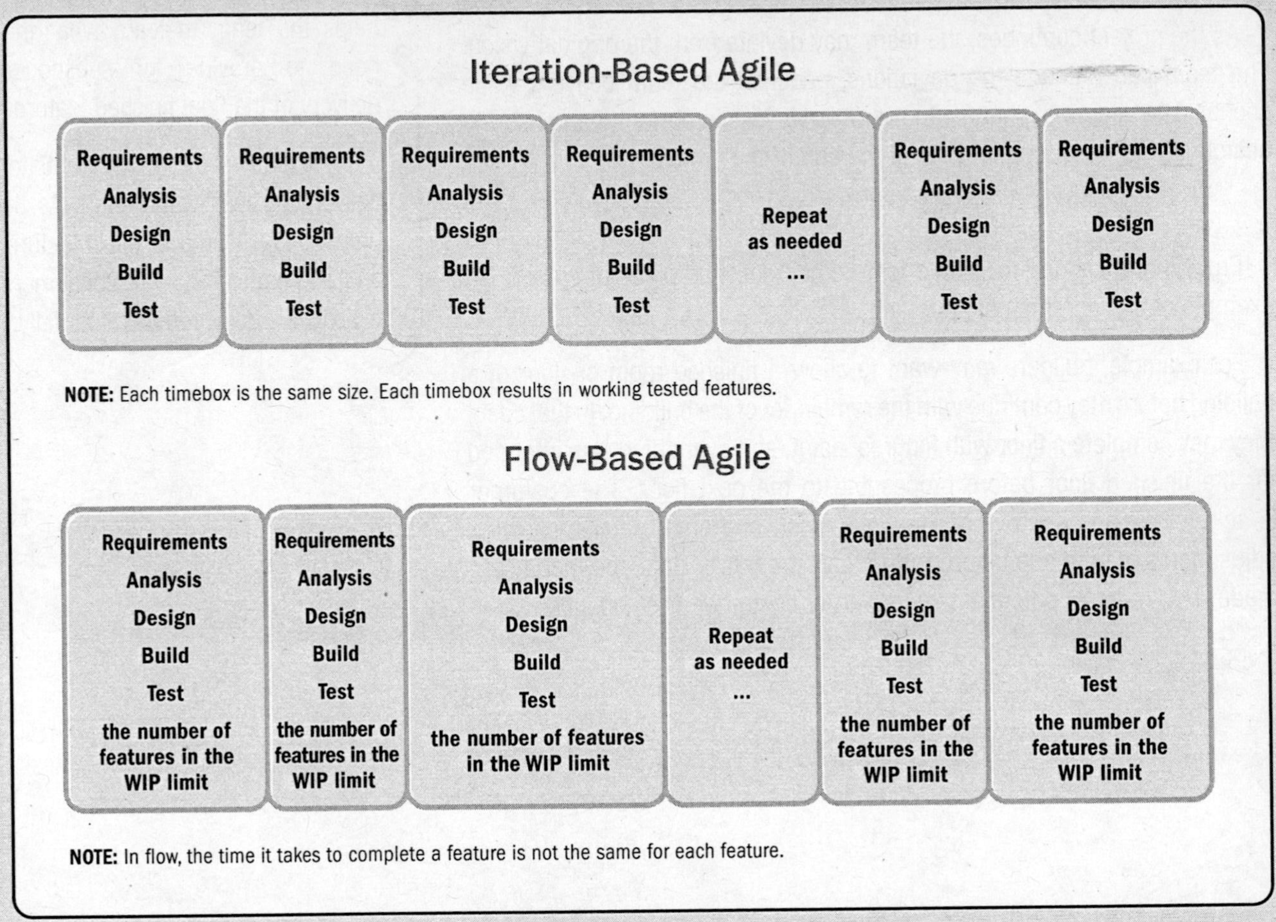

Iteration-Based Agile

Requirements	Requirements	Requirements	Requirements		Requirements	Requirements
Analysis	Analysis	Analysis	Analysis	Repeat as needed ...	Analysis	Analysis
Design	Design	Design	Design		Design	Design
Build	Build	Build	Build		Build	Build
Test	Test	Test	Test		Test	Test

NOTE: Each timebox is the same size. Each timebox results in working tested features.

Flow-Based Agile

Requirements	Requirements	Requirements		Requirements	Requirements
Analysis	Analysis	Analysis	Repeat as needed ...	Analysis	Analysis
Design	Design	Design		Design	Design
Build	Build	Build		Build	Build
Test	Test	Test		Test	Test
the number of features in the WIP limit	the number of features in the WIP limit	the number of features in the WIP limit		the number of features in the WIP limit	the number of features in the WIP limit

NOTE: In flow, the time it takes to complete a feature is not the same for each feature.

Figure 3-5. Iteration-Based and Flow-Based Agile Life Cycles

In iteration-based agile, the team works in iterations (timeboxes of equal duration) to deliver completed features. The team works on the most important feature, collaborating as a team to finish it. Then the team works on the next most important feature and finishes it. The team may decide to work on a few features at a time, but the team does not address all of the work for the iteration at once (i.e., does not address all of the requirements, followed by all of the analyses, etc.).

In flow-based agile, the team pulls features from the backlog based on its capacity to start work rather than on an iteration-based schedule. The team defines its workflow with columns on a task board and manages the work in progress for each column. Each feature may take a different amount of time to finish. Teams keep work-in-progress sizes small to better identify issues early and reduce rework should changes be required. Without iterations to define planning and review points, the team and business stakeholders determine the most appropriate schedule for planning, product reviews, and retrospectives.

Agile life cycles are those that fulfill the principles of the Agile Manifesto. In particular, customer satisfaction increases with early and continuous delivery of valuable products. Moreover, an incremental deliverable that is functional and provides value is the primary measure of progress. Agile life cycles combine both iterative and incremental approaches in order to adapt to high degrees of change and deliver project value more often.

3.1.5 AGILE SUITABILITY FILTERS

Various assessment models exist to help determine the likely fit or gaps for using agile approaches. These models assess project and organizational factors associated with adoption and suitability and then provide scores indicating alignment or potential risk areas. Appendix X3 provides a synthesis of popular assessment models for use as an agile suitability filter.

3.1.6 CHARACTERISTICS OF HYBRID LIFE CYCLES

It is not necessary to use a single approach for an entire project. Projects often combine elements of different life cycles in order to achieve certain goals. A combination of predictive, iterative, incremental, and/or agile approaches is a hybrid approach.

Figure 3-6 depicts the basic, pure approaches to project types that combine to form a hybrid model. The early processes utilize an agile development life cycle, which is then followed by a predictive rollout phase. This approach can be used when there is uncertainty, complexity, and risk in the development portion of the project that would benefit from an agile approach, followed by a defined, repeatable rollout phase that is appropriate to undertake in a predictive way, perhaps by a different team. An example of this approach is the development of a new high-tech product followed by rollout and training to thousands of users.

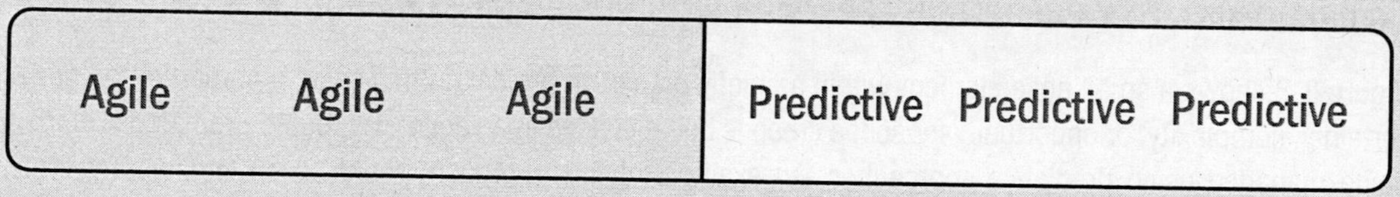

Agile	Agile	Agile	Predictive	Predictive	Predictive

Figure 3-6. Agile Development Followed by a Predictive Rollout

3.1.7 COMBINED AGILE AND PREDICTIVE APPROACHES

Another approach is to use a combination of agile and predictive approaches throughout the life cycle.

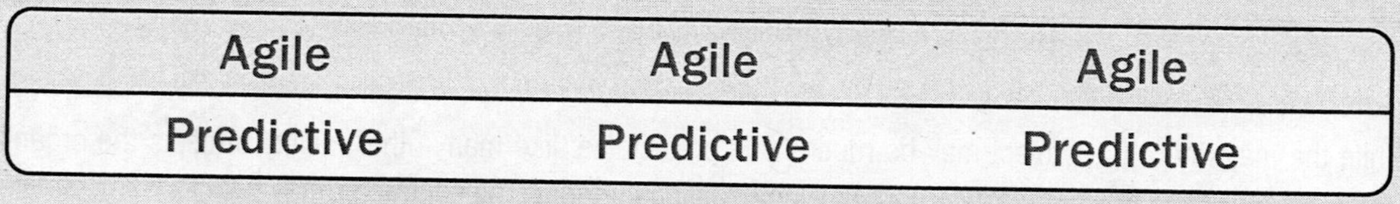

Agile	Agile	Agile
Predictive	Predictive	Predictive

Figure 3-7. A Combined Agile and Predictive Approach Used Simultaneously

In Figure 3-7, a combination of both predictive and agile approaches are used in the same project. Perhaps the team is incrementally transitioning to agile and using some approaches like short iterations, daily standups, and retrospectives, but other aspects of the project such as upfront estimation, work assignment, and progress tracking are still following predictive approaches.

Using both predictive and agile approaches is a common scenario. It would be misleading to call the approach agile since it clearly does not fully embody the agile mindset, values, and principles. However, it would also be inaccurate to call it predictive since it is a hybrid approach.

3.1.8 PREDOMINANTLY PREDICTIVE APPROACH WITH SOME AGILE COMPONENTS

Figure 3-8 shows a small agile element within a chiefly predictive project. In this case, a portion of the project with uncertainty, complexity, or opportunity for scope creep is being tackled in an agile way, but the remainder of the project is being managed using predictive approaches. An example of this approach would be an engineering firm that is building a facility with a new component.

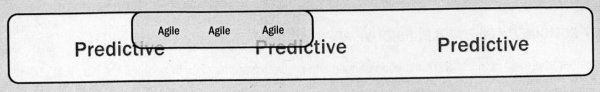

Figure 3-8. A Largely Predictive Approach with Agile Components

While the majority of the project may be routine and predictable, like many other facility projects the organization has undertaken before, this project incorporates a new roofing material. The contractor may plan for some small-scale installation trials on the ground first to determine the best installation method and to uncover issues early while there is plenty of time to solve them and incrementally improve processes through experimentation and adaptation.

3.1.9 A LARGELY AGILE APPROACH WITH A PREDICTIVE COMPONENT

Figure 3-9 depicts a largely agile approach with a predictive component. This approach might be used when a particular element is non-negotiable or not executable using an agile approach. Examples include integrating an external component developed by a different vendor that cannot or will not partner in a collaborative or incremental way. A single integration is required after the component is delivered.

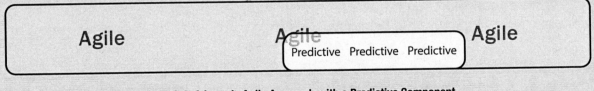

Figure 3-9. A Largely Agile Approach with a Predictive Component

A government department had a credit insurance application development project. The multi-year project was to replace its aging underwriting system with a new, more responsive user interface and system integrations. The bulk of the project was undertaken using an agile approach with continual business input.

The premium rate calculations were handed down from the Organisation for Economic Co-operation and Development (OECD) as a 200-page specification. The steps were very clearly explained with little opportunity for confusion (or interim result confirmation by the business) and were coded up by a separate team working its way through the calculation steps. The two teams collaborated on the input variables required for the calculation and how to consume and display the output values, but beyond that, the calculation team worked in a largely predictive manner.

When the calculation team's portion was complete, the outputs from the premium rate calculations were displayed on the screens and in the reports. Then the business users provided feedback on the appearance and use of the information. The two teams ran concurrently, but had little need for interaction. Having them physically close to each other made it easier to check in on development progress, but largely they were separate subprojects.

3.1.10 HYBRID LIFE CYCLES AS FIT-FOR-PURPOSE

Project teams may design a hybrid life cycle based on project risks. For example, a campus construction project may have multiple buildings to improve and build. An incremental approach would focus resources on completing some buildings earlier than others, accelerating the return on investment. Each individual delivery may be sufficiently well known to benefit from a predictive life cycle for that building alone.

The goal of project management is to produce business value in the best possible way given the current environment. It does not matter if that way is agile or predictive. The question to ask is: "How can we be most successful?"

Is feedback needed as the team produces value? If so, increments will help. Is it necessary to manage risk as ideas are explored? If so, iterations or agile will help.

When the organization cannot deliver intermediate value, agile approaches may not be useful. That is okay—agile for the sake of agile is not the goal. The point is to select a life cycle or a combination of life cycles that work for the project, the risks, and the culture.

Agile is about customer-based delivery on a frequent basis. That delivery creates feedback for the team. The team uses that feedback to plan and replan the next chunk of work.

3.1.11 HYBRID LIFE CYCLES AS TRANSITION STRATEGY

Many teams are not able to make the switch to agile ways of working overnight. Agile techniques look and feel very different to those who are accustomed to and have been successful in a predictive environment. The larger the organization and the more moving parts, the longer it will take to transition. For that reason, it makes sense to plan a gradual transition.

A gradual transition involves adding more iterative techniques to improve learning and alignment among teams and stakeholders. Later, consider adding more incremental techniques to accelerate value and return on investment to sponsors. This combination of various approaches is considered a hybrid approach.

Try these new techniques on a less risky project with a medium- to low-degree of uncertainty. Then, when the organization is successful with a hybrid approach, try more complex projects that require more of those techniques to be added. This is a way to tailor the progressive hybrid transition to the organization's situation and specific risks and the team's readiness to adapt and embrace the changes.

3.2 MIXING AGILE APPROACHES

Agile teams rarely limit their practices to one agile approach. Each project context has its own peculiarities, such as the varied mix of team member skills and backgrounds; the various components of the product under development; and the age, scale, criticality, complexity, and regulatory constraints of the environment in which the work takes place.

Agile frameworks are not customized for the team. The team may need to tailor practices to deliver value on a regular basis. Often, teams practice their own special blend of agile, even if they use a particular framework as a starting point.

BLENDING APPROACHES

As an example of tailoring agile frameworks, one of the most common blends in widespread use involves a coordinated use of the Scrum framework, the Kanban Method, and elements of the eXtreme Programming (XP) method. Scrum provides guidance on the use of a product backlog, a product owner, scrum master, and a cross-functional development team, including sprint planning, daily scrum, sprint review, and sprint retrospective sessions. A kanban board helps the team to further improve its effectiveness by visualizing the flow of work, making impediments easily visible, and allowing flow to be managed by adjusting work in process limits. In addition, XP-inspired engineering practices such as use of story cards, continuous integration, refactoring, automated testing, and test-driven development further increase the effectiveness of the agile team. In summary, the blend of practices from these various sources produces a synergistic result of higher performance than each individual component in isolation.

3.3 PROJECT FACTORS THAT INFLUENCE TAILORING

Sometimes project attributes require tailoring an approach for a better fit. Table 3-2 identifies some project factors and tailoring options to consider.

Table 3-2. Tailoring Options to Improve Fit

Project Factor	Tailoring Options
Demand pattern: steady or sporadic	Many teams find that using a cadence (in the form of a regular timebox) helps them demo, retrospect, and take in new work. In addition, some teams need more flexibility in their acceptance of more work. Teams can use flow-based agile with a cadence to get the best of both worlds.
Rate of process improvement required by the level of team experience	Retrospect more often and select improvements.
The flow of work is often interrupted by various delays or impediments	Consider making work visible using kanban boards and experimenting with limits for the various areas of the work process in order to improve flow.
The quality of the product increments is poor	Consider using the various test-driven development practices. This mistake-proofing discipline makes it difficult for defects to remain undetected.
More than one team is needed to build a product	To scale from one to several agile teams, with minimal disruption, first learn about agile program management or formal scaling frameworks. Then, craft an approach that fits the project context.
The project team members are inexperienced in the use of agile approaches	Consider starting by training team members in the fundamentals of the agile mindset and principles. If the team decides to use a specific approach such as Scrum or Kanban, provide a workshop on that approach so the team members can learn how to use it.

For additional guidance on factors that influence tailoring see Appendix X2 on Attributes that Influence Tailoring.

4

IMPLEMENTING AGILE: CREATING AN AGILE ENVIRONMENT

4.1 START WITH AN AGILE MINDSET

Managing a project using an agile approach requires that the project team adopt an agile mindset. The answers to the following questions will help to develop an implementation strategy:

◆ How can the project team act in an agile manner?

◆ What can the team deliver quickly and obtain early feedback to benefit the next delivery cycle?

◆ How can the team act in a transparent manner?

◆ What work can be avoided in order to focus on high-priority items?

◆ How can a servant-leadership approach benefit the achievement of the team's goals?

4.2 SERVANT LEADERSHIP EMPOWERS THE TEAM

Agile approaches emphasize servant leadership as a way to empower teams. Servant leadership is the practice of leading through service to the team, by focusing on understanding and addressing the needs and development of team members in order to enable the highest possible team performance.

The role of a servant leader is to facilitate the team's discovery and definition of agile. Servant leaders practice and radiate agile. Servant leaders approach project work in this order:

◆ **Purpose.** Work with the team to define the "why" or purpose so they can engage and coalesce around the goal for the project. The entire team optimizes at the project level, not the person level.

◆ **People.** Once the purpose is established, encourage the team to create an environment where everyone can succeed. Ask each team member to contribute across the project work.

◆ **Process.** Do not plan on following the "perfect" agile process, but instead look for the results. When a cross-functional team delivers finished value often and reflects on the product and process, the teams are agile. It does not matter what the team calls its process.

The following characteristics of servant leadership enable project leaders to become more agile and facilitate the team's success:

◆ Promoting self-awareness;

◆ Listening;

◆ Serving those on the team;

◆ Helping people grow;

◆ Coaching vs. controlling;

◆ Promoting safety, respect, and trust; and

◆ Promoting the energy and intelligence of others.

Servant leadership is not unique to agile. But once having practiced it, servant leaders can usually see how well servant leadership integrates into the agile mindset and value.

When leaders develop their servant leadership or facilitative skills, they are more likely to become agile. As a result, servant leaders can help their teams collaborate to deliver value faster.

Successful agile teams embrace the growth mindset, where people believe they can learn new skills. When the team and the servant leaders believe they can all learn, everyone becomes more capable.

4.2.1 SERVANT LEADER RESPONSIBILITIES

Servant leaders manage relationships to build communication and coordination within the team and across the organization. These relationships help the leaders navigate the organization to support the team. This kind of support helps to remove impediments and facilitates the team to streamline its processes. Because servant leaders understand agile and practice a specific approach to agile, they can assist in fulfilling the team's needs.

4.2.1.1 SERVANT LEADERS FACILITATE

When project managers act as servant leaders, the emphasis shifts from "managing coordination" to "facilitating collaboration." Facilitators help everyone do their best thinking and work. Facilitators encourage the team's participation, understanding, and shared responsibility for the team's output. Facilitators help the team create acceptable solutions.

Servant leaders promote collaboration and conversation within the team and between teams. For example, a servant leader helps to expose and communicate bottlenecks inside and between teams. Then the teams resolve those bottlenecks.

Additionally, a facilitator encourages collaboration through interactive meetings, informal dialog, and knowledge sharing. Servant leaders do this by becoming impartial bridge-builders and coaches, rather than by making decisions for which others should be responsible.

4.2.1.2 SERVANT LEADERS REMOVE ORGANIZATIONAL IMPEDIMENTS

The first value of the Agile Manifesto is individuals and interactions over processes and tools. What better responsibility for a servant leader to take on than to take a hard look at processes that are impeding a team's or organization's agility and work to streamline them? For example, if a department requires extensive documentation, the role of the servant leader could be to work with that department to review required documentation, assist with creating a shared understanding of how agile deliverables meet those requirements, and evaluate the amount of documentation required so teams are spending more time delivering a valuable product instead of producing exhaustive documentation.

Servant leaders should also look at other processes that are lengthy, causing bottlenecks and impeding a team's or organization's agility. Examples of processes or departments that may need to be addressed include finance, change control boards, or audits. Servant leaders can partner and work with others to challenge them to review their processes to support agile teams and leaders. For example, what good is it for the team to deliver working product every 2 weeks only to have the product fall into a queue or process that could take 6 or more weeks to release due to lengthy release processes? Far too many organizations have these "bottleneck" processes that prevent teams from quickly delivering valuable products or services. The servant leader has the ability to change or remove these organizational impediments to support delivery teams.

INTERPERSONAL SKILLS VERSUS TECHNICAL SKILLS

In addition to servant leadership, team members emphasize their interpersonal and emotional intelligence skills—not just technical skills. Everyone on the team works to exhibit more initiative, integrity, emotional intelligence, honesty, collaboration, humility, and willingness to communicate in various ways so that the entire team can work together well.

The team needs these skills so they can respond well to changes in project direction and technical product changes. When everyone can adapt to the work and to each other, the entire team is more likely to succeed.

4.2.1.3 SERVANT LEADERS PAVE THE WAY FOR OTHERS' CONTRIBUTION

In agile, the team manages its work process and its work product. That self-management and self-organization applies to everyone serving and supporting the organization and project. Servant leaders work to fulfill the needs of the teams, projects, and organization. Servant leaders may work with facilities for a team space, work with management to enable the team to focus on one project at a time, or work with the product owner to develop stories with the team. Some servant leaders work with auditors to refine the processes needed in regulatory environments, and some servant leaders work with the finance department to transition the organization to incremental budgeting.

The servant leader focuses on paving the way for the team to do its best work. The servant leader influences projects and encourages the organization to think differently.

4.2.1.4 CONSIDER THESE SERVANT LEADER RESPONSIBILITIES

Servant leaders can have many possible titles, but what is most important is what they do. Here are some examples of the responsibilities a servant leader may have:

◆ Educate stakeholders around why and how to be agile. Explain the benefits of business value based on prioritization, greater accountability and productivity of empowered teams, and improved quality from more frequent reviews, etc.

◆ Support the team through mentoring, encouragement, and support. Advocate for team members training and career development. The oxymoronic quote "We lead teams by standing behind them" speaks to the role of the leader in developing their team members. Through support, encouragement, and professional development, team members gain confidence, take on larger roles, and contribute at higher levels within their organizations. A key role of the servant leader is to nurture and grow team members through and beyond their current roles, even if that means losing them from the team.

◆ Help the team with technical project management activities like quantitative risk analysis. Sometimes team members may not have knowledge or experience in roles or functions. Servant leaders who may have more exposure or training in techniques can support the team by providing training or undertaking these activities.

◆ Celebrate team successes and support and bridge building activities with external groups. Create upward spirals of appreciation and good will for increased collaboration.

4.2.2 ROLE OF THE PROJECT MANAGER IN AN AGILE ENVIRONMENT

The role of the project manager in an agile project is somewhat of an unknown, because many agile frameworks and approaches do not address the role of the project manager. Some agile practitioners think the role of a project manager is not needed, due to self-organizing teams taking on the former responsibilities of the project manager. However, pragmatic agile practitioners and organizations realize that project managers can add significant value in many situations. The key difference is that their roles and responsibilities look somewhat different.

TIP

The value of project managers is not in their position, but in their ability to make everyone else better.

4.2.3 PROJECT MANAGERS USE SERVANT LEADERSHIP

The *PMBOK® Guide – Sixth Edition*, defines the project manager as "the person assigned by the performing organization to lead the team that is responsible for achieving the project objectives."

Many project managers are accustomed to being at the center of coordination for the project, tracking and representing the team's status to the rest of the organization. This approach was fine when projects were decomposed into siloed functions.

However, in high-change projects, there is more complexity than one person can manage. Instead, cross-functional teams coordinate their own work and collaborate with the business representative (the product owner).

When working on an agile project, project managers shift from being the center to serving the team and the management. In an agile environment, project managers are servant leaders, changing their emphasis to coaching people who want help, fostering greater collaboration on the team, and aligning stakeholder needs. As a servant leader, project managers encourage the distribution of responsibility to the team: to those people who have the knowledge to get work done.

4.3 TEAM COMPOSITION

A core tenet in both the values and the principles of the Agile Manifesto is the importance of individuals and interactions. Agile optimizes the flow of value, emphasizing rapid feature delivery to the customer, rather than on how people are "utilized."

TIP

Build projects around motivated individuals. Give them the environment and support they need and trust them to get the job done.

When teams think about how to optimize the flow of value, the following benefits become apparent:

- People are more likely to collaborate.

- Teams finish valuable work faster.

- Teams waste much less time because they do not multitask and have to re-establish context.

4.3.1 AGILE TEAMS

Agile teams focus on rapid product development so they can obtain feedback. In practice, the most effective agile teams tend to range in size from three to nine members. Ideally, agile teams are colocated in a team space. Team members are 100% dedicated to the teams. Agile encourages self-managing teams, where team members decide who will perform the work within the next period's defined scope. Agile teams thrive with servant leadership. The leaders support the teams' approach to their work.

Cross-functional agile teams produce functional product increments frequently. That is because the teams collectively own the work and together have all of the necessary skills to deliver completed work.

Regardless of the overall agile approach, the more a team limits its work in progress, the more likely its members can collaborate to expedite work across the board. Team members in successful agile teams work to collaborate in various ways (such as pairing, swarming, and mobbing) so they do not fall into the trap of mini-waterfalls instead of collaborative work. Mini-waterfalls occur when the team addresses *all* of the requirements in a given period, then attempts to do *all* of the design, then moves on to do *all* of the building. Using this scenario, at some point in the building or the testing following the building, the team may realize it had assumptions that are no longer valid. In this case, the team wasted time in addressing *all* of the requirements. Instead, when team members collaborate to produce a small number of features across the board, they learn as they proceed and deliver smaller finished features.

Agile projects benefit from project team structures that improve collaboration within and among the teams. Table 4-1 shows how collaborative team members boost productivity and facilitate innovative problem solving.

Table 4-1. Attributes of Successful Agile Teams

Attribute	Goal
Dedicated people	• Increased focus and productivity • Small team, fewer than ten people
Cross-functional team members	• Develop and deliver often • Deliver finished value as an independent team • Integrate all the work activities to deliver finished work • Provide feedback from inside the team and from others, such as the product owner
Colocation or ability to manage any location challenges	• Better communication • Improved team dynamics • Knowledge sharing • Reduced cost of learning • Able to commit to working with each other
Mixed team of generalists and specialists	• Specialists provide dedicated expertise and generalists provide flexibility of who does what • Team brings their specialist capabilities and often become generalizing specialists, with a focus specialty plus breadth of experience across multiple skills
Stable work environment	• Depend on each other to deliver • Agreed-upon approach to the work • Simplified team cost calculations (run rate) • Preservation and expansion of intellectual capital

4.3.2 AGILE ROLES

In agile, three common roles are used:

◆ Cross-functional team members,

◆ Product owner, and

◆ Team facilitator.

Table 4-2 describes these team roles.

Table 4-2. Agile Team Roles

Role	Description
Cross-functional team member	Cross-functional teams consist of team members with all the skills necessary to produce a working product. In software development, cross-functional teams are typically comprised of designers, developers, testers, and any other required roles. The cross-functional development teams consist of professionals who deliver potentially releasable product on a regular cadence. Cross-functional teams are critical because they can deliver finished work in the shortest possible time, with higher quality, without external dependencies.
Product owner	The product owner is responsible for guiding the direction of the product. Product owners rank the work based on its business value. Product owners work with their teams daily by providing product feedback and setting direction on the next piece of functionality to be developed/delivered. That means the work is small, often small enough to be described on one index card. The product owner works with stakeholders, customers, and the teams to define the product direction. Typically, product owners have a business background and bring deep subject matter expertise to the decisions. Sometimes, the product owner requests help from people with deep domain expertise, such as architects, or deep customer expertise, such as product managers. Product owners need training on how to organize and manage the flow of work through the team. In agile, the product owners create the backlog for and with the team. The backlog helps the teams see how to deliver the highest value without creating waste. A critical success factor for agile teams is strong product ownership. Without attention to the highest value for the customer, the agile team may create features that are not appreciated, or otherwise insufficiently valuable, therefore wasting effort.
Team facilitator	The third role typically seen on agile teams is of a team facilitator, a servant leader. This role may be called a project manager, scrum master, project team lead, team coach, or team facilitator. All agile teams need servant leadership on the team. People need time to build their servant leadership skills of facilitation, coaching, and impediment removal. Initially, many organizations invite external agile coaches to help them when their internal coaching capability is not yet fully developed. External coaches have the advantage of experience, but the disadvantage of weak relationships in the client organization. Internal coaches, on the other hand, have strong relationships in their organization, but may lack the breadth of experience that would make them highly effective.

4.3.3 GENERALIZING SPECIALISTS

Agile teams are cross-functional, but the people often do not start off that way. However, many successful agile teams are made up of generalizing specialists, or "T-shaped" people.

This means team members have both a focus specialty plus a breadth of experience across multiple skills, rather than a single specialization. Agile team members work to develop such characteristics due to intense collaboration and self-organization to swarm and get work done quickly, which requires them to routinely help each other.

A single person's throughput is not relevant. Focusing on a single person's throughput may even be harmful if it creates a bottleneck for the rest of the team. The goal is for the *team* to optimize the delivery of finished work to get feedback.

If the customer desires great results, such as rapid feature delivery with excellent quality, the team cannot be structured just with specialist roles in an attempt to maximize resource efficiency. The team's objective is flow efficiency, optimizing the throughput of the entire team. Small batch sizes promote working together as a team. The product owner's job is to make sure the team works on the highest-value work.

4.3.4 TEAM STRUCTURES

Teams have adopted agile principles and practices across many industries. They organize people into cross-functional teams to iteratively develop working products.

● ● ● ● ●

C A S E

The core team assembled to write this practice guide had varied backgrounds—some represented PMI and some represented Agile Alliance. They were self-organizing and worked in increments to complete the work. PMI assembled a group of subject matter experts to inspect the work, and this allowed the team to incorporate feedback and improve the product as it was developed. However the core team was not representative of a typical agile team because its members' time was not 100% dedicated to this endeavor.

● ● ● ● ●

Some organizations have been able to create colocated, cross-functional teams; others have a different situation. Instead of having all team members colocated, some organizations have distributed or dispersed teams. Distributed teams have cross-functional teams in different locations. Dispersed teams may have each team member working in a completely different location, either in an office or from home. While these arrangements are not ideal due to increased communication costs, they may still be workable.

In one large, U.S.-based financial institution there was a program with a set of teams where the team members were based on the East Coast of the United States and several locations throughout India. When the team first started, it was one large dispersed team (UX, analysts, developers, and testers) doing a "follow the sun"[2] development practice where some working time overlapped across the team members to do warm hand-offs with the work. Team members conducted daily standups together and used webcams to include all team members. Key roles (analysts, product owners, UX designers, and development leads) in the U.S. would come in early to answer any questions from their India-based team members and help to resolve impediments.

As the product started getting larger, and more funding came through, they decided to break into five smaller teams. To do this, they decided to build colocated, distributed teams in various locations. They made the decision to build cross-functional, colocated teams in each of these locations consisting of developers and testers.

They also had a core set of analysts, based in the two U.S. locations, who worked with their U.S.-based product manager and product owners and then worked with each of the teams, respectively. Although they had some structure in place where they conducted product reviews as an entire program, most of the other activities were conducted at a team level, based on what worked best for each team, to allow them to self-organize.

4.3.5 DEDICATED TEAM MEMBERS

What happens when the team members' time is not 100% dedicated to the team? While this condition is not ideal, unfortunately, it sometimes cannot be avoided.

The key problem with having someone invest only a capacity of 25% or 50% on the team is that they will multitask and task switch. Multitasking reduces the throughput of the team's work and impacts the team's ability to predict delivery consistently.

TIP

Multitasking slows the progress of the entire team, because team members waste time context switching and/or waiting for each other to finish other work. When people are 100% dedicated to the team, the team has the fastest possible throughput.

[2] A follow-the-sun development process is one where work is handed off at the end of every day from one site to the next, many time zones away in order to speed up product development.

People experience productivity losses somewhere between 20% and 40% when task switching. The loss increases exponentially with the number of tasks.

When a person multitasks between two projects, that person is not 50% on each project. Instead, due to the cost of task switching, the person is somewhere between 20% and 40% on each project.

People are more likely to make mistakes when they multitask. Task-switching consumes working memory and people are less likely to remember their context when they multitask.

When everyone on the team is 100% allocated to one project, they can continuously collaborate as a team, making everyone's work more effective.

●●●○○

CASE

Since core team members developing this practice guide cannot dedicate 100% of their capacity to the team's efforts, their throughput is substantially lower than what it might be if they could afford to collocate and invest their attention full-time to the project. However, while it is economically viable to collaborate, even if dispersed and operating at a fraction of their full capacity, it is not feasible to colocate and focus at full capacity. Therefore, the team identified their dispersion as a potential risk. The team tracks and monitors the progress of their work through the use of collaborative tools and adjusts assignments based on individual capacity accordingly.

○○○●●

See Table A1-2 on Project Management Process Group and Knowledge Area Mapping for more tips on teams in agile environments, specifically the processes in the Project Resource Management Knowledge Area.

TIP ▶

Not all teams have all the roles that they need. For example, some teams need support from database administrators or research analysts. When a team has temporarily assigned specialists, it is important to ensure that everyone has the same set of expectations. Is this specialist 100% allocated to the team and for how long? Set expectations with everyone (the specialist and the team) to clarify the level of commitment so the team can deliver. Part-time assignments create risks for the project.

4.3.6 TEAM WORKSPACES

Teams need a space in which they can work together, to understand their state as a team, and to collaborate. Some agile teams all work in one room together. Some teams have a team workspace for their standups and charts, and work on their own in cubicles or offices.

While companies are moving toward open, collaborative work environments, organizations also need to create quiet spaces for workers who need uninterrupted time to think and work. Therefore, companies are designing their offices to balance common and social areas (sometimes called "caves and common") with quiet areas or private spaces where individuals can work without being interrupted.

When teams have geographically distributed members, the team decides how much of their workplace is virtual and how much is physical. Technology such as document sharing, video conferencing, and other virtual collaboration tools help people collaborate remotely.

Geographically distributed teams need virtual workspaces. In addition, consider getting the team together in person at regular intervals so the team can build trust and learn how to work together.

Some techniques to consider for managing communication in dispersed teams are *fishbowl windows* and *remote pairing*:

◆ Create a fishbowl window by setting up long-lived video conferencing links between the various locations in which the team is dispersed. People start the link at the beginning of a workday, and close it at the end. In this way, people can see and engage spontaneously with each other, reducing the collaboration lag otherwise inherent in the geographical separation.

◆ Set up remote pairing by using virtual conferencing tools to share screens, including voice and video links. As long as the time zone differences are accounted for, this may prove almost as effective as face-to-face pairing.

TIP

Form teams by bringing people with different skills from different functions together. Educate managers and leaders about the agile mindset and engage them early in the agile transformation.

4.3.7 OVERCOMING ORGANIZATIONAL SILOS

The best place to start when forming agile teams is by building a foundational trust and a safe work environment to ensure that all team members have an equal voice and can be heard and considered. This, along with building the agile mindset is the underlying success factor—all other challenges and risks can be mitigated.

Often, siloed organizations create impediments for forming cross-functional agile teams. The team members needed to build the cross-functional teams typically report to different managers and have different metrics by which managers measure their performance. Managers need to focus on flow efficiency (and team-based metrics) rather than resource efficiency.

To overcome organizational silos, work with the various managers of these team members and have them dedicate the necessary individuals to the cross-functional team. This not only creates team synergy but also allows the organization to see how leveraging its people will optimize the project or product being built.

For more information about teams see Appendix X2 on Attributes that Influence Tailoring.

TIP *As an agile project leader, first focus on how you can create a team that is cross-functional and 100% dedicated to one team. Even if it means just getting key team members, such as the developers and testers, to work and communicate together on a daily basis, that is a step in the right direction toward agility.*

5

IMPLEMENTING AGILE: DELIVERING IN AN AGILE ENVIRONMENT

5.1 CHARTER THE PROJECT AND THE TEAM

Every project needs a project charter so the project team knows why this project matters, where the team is headed and what the project objective is. However, the project charter itself may not be enough for the team. Agile teams require team norms and an understanding of how to work together. In that case, the team might need a team charter.

The chartering process helps the team learn how to work together and coalesce around the project.

At a minimum, for an agile project, the team needs the project vision or purpose and a clear set of working agreements. An agile project charter answers these questions:

◆ Why are we doing this project? This is the project vision.

◆ Who benefits and how? This may be part of the project vision and/or project purpose.

◆ What does done mean for the project? These are the project's release criteria.

◆ How are we going to work together? This explains the intended flow of work.

A servant leader may facilitate the chartering process. A team can coalesce by working together, and the project charter is a great way to start working. In addition, team members may want to collaborate to understand how they will work together.

Teams do not need a formal process for chartering as long as the teams understand how to work together. Some teams benefit from a team chartering process. Here are some chartering ideas for team members to use as a basis for their social contract:

◆ Team values, such as sustainable pace and core hours;

◆ Working agreements, such as what "ready" means so the team can take in work; what "done" means so the team can judge completeness consistently; respecting the timebox; or the use of work-in-process limits;

◆ Ground rules, such as one person talking in a meeting; and

◆ Group norms, such as how the team treats meeting times.

The servant leader together with the team may decide to address other behaviors.

Remember that the team's social contract—its team charter—is how the team members interact with each other. The goal of the team charter is to create an agile environment in which team members can work to the best of their ability as a team.

5.2 COMMON AGILE PRACTICES

Sections 5.2.1 through 5.2.8 describe a few of the most common agile project practices.

5.2.1 RETROSPECTIVES

The single most important practice is the retrospective because it allows the team to learn about, improve, and adapt its process.

Retrospectives help the team learn from its previous work on the product and its process. One of the principles behind the Agile Manifesto is: "At regular intervals, the team reflects on how to become more effective, then tunes and adjusts its behavior accordingly."

Many teams use iterations—especially 2-week iterations—because the iteration prompts a demonstration and a retrospective at the end. However, the team does not need iterations in order to retrospect. Team members may decide to retrospect at these key times:

◆ When the team completes a release or ships something. It does not have to be a monumental increment. It can be any release, no matter how small.

◆ When more than a few weeks have passed since the previous retrospective.

◆ When the team appears to be stuck and completed work is not flowing through the team.

◆ When the team reaches any other milestone.

Teams benefit from allocating enough time to learn, either from an interim retrospective or an end-of-the-project retrospective. Teams need to learn about their work product and work process. For example, some teams have trouble finishing work. When teams plan enough time, they can structure their retrospective to gather data, process that data, and decide what to try later as an experiment.

First and foremost, a retrospective is not about blame; the retrospective is a time for the team to learn from previous work and make small improvements.

The retrospective is about looking at the qualitative (people's feelings) and quantitative (measurements) data, then using that data to find root causes, designing countermeasures, and developing action plans. The project team may end up with many action items to remove impediments.

Consider limiting the number of action items to the team's capacity to address improvement in the upcoming iteration or work period. Trying to improve too many things at once and not finishing any of them is much worse than planning to complete fewer items and successfully completing all of them. Then, when time allows, the team can work on the next improvement opportunity on the list. When the team selects the improvements, decide how to measure the outcomes. Then, in the next time period, measure the outcomes to validate success or failure of each improvement.

A facilitator from the team leads them through an activity to rank the importance of each improvement item. Once the improvement items are ranked by the team, the team chooses the appropriate number to work on for the next iteration (or adds work to the flow if flow-based).

5.2.2 BACKLOG PREPARATION

The backlog is the ordered list of all the work, presented in story form, for a team. There is no need to create all of the stories for the entire project before the work starts—only enough to understand the first release in broad brushstrokes and then sufficient items for the next iteration.

Product owners (or a product owner value team that includes the product manager and all relevant product owners for that area of the product,) might produce a product roadmap to show the anticipated sequence of deliverables over time. The product owner replans the roadmap based on what the team produces. (See Appendix X3 on Agile Suitability Filter Tools for examples of roadmaps.)

5.2.3 BACKLOG REFINEMENT

In iteration-based agile, the product owner often works with the team to prepare some stories for the upcoming iteration during one or more sessions in the middle of the iteration. The purpose of these meetings is to refine enough stories so the team understands what the stories are and how large the stories are in relation to each other.

There is no consensus on how long the refinement should be. There is a continuum of:

◆ Just-in-time refinement for flow-based agile. The team takes the next card off the to-do column and discusses it.

◆ Many iteration-based agile teams use a timeboxed 1-hour discussion midway through a 2-week iteration. (The team selects an iteration duration that provides them frequent-enough feedback.)

◆ Multiple refinement discussions for iteration-based agile teams. Teams can use this when they are new to the product, the product area, or the problem domain.

> **TIP** *Consider using impact mapping to see how the product fits together. Under normal circumstances, the product owner leads this work. A servant leader can facilitate any necessary meetings as a way of serving the project.*

Refinement meetings allow the product owner to present story ideas to the team and for the team to learn about the potential challenges or problems in the stories. If the product owner is unsure of the dependencies, the product owner can request the team to spike the feature in order to understand the risks.

There are many ways for the product owner to conduct backlog preparation and refinement meetings, including for example:

◆ Encourage the team to work as triads of developer, tester, business analyst/product owner to discuss and write the story.

◆ Present the overall story concept to the team. The team discusses and refines it into as many stories as required.

◆ Work with the team to find various ways to explore and write the stories together, making sure all of the stories are small enough so the team can produce a steady flow of completed work. Consider becoming able to complete a story at least once a day.

Teams often have a goal of spending not more than 1 hour per week refining stories for the next batch of work. Teams want to maximize the time spent doing work as opposed to planning work. If the team needs to spend more than 1 hour per week refining stories, the product owner could be overpreparing, or the team may be lacking some critical skills needed to evaluate and refine the work.

5.2.4 DAILY STANDUPS

Teams use standups to microcommit to each other, uncover problems, and ensure the work flows smoothly through the team.

Timebox the standup to no longer than 15 minutes. The team "walks" the Kanban or task board in some way, and anyone from the team can facilitate the standup.

In iteration-based agile, everyone answers the following questions in a round-robin fashion:

◆ What did I complete since the last standup?

◆ What am I planning to complete between now and the next standup?

◆ What are my impediments (or risks or problems)?

Questions like these generate answers that allow the team to self-organize and hold each other accountable for completing the work they committed to the day before and throughout the iteration.

Flow-based agile has a different approach to standups, focusing on the team's throughput. The team assesses the board from right to left. The questions are:

◆ What do we need to do to advance this piece of work?

◆ Is anyone working on anything that is not on the board?

◆ What do we need to finish as a team?

◆ Are there any bottlenecks or blockers to the flow of work?

One of the antipatterns typically seen in standups is they become status meetings. Teams who have traditionally worked in a predictive environment may tend to fall into this antipattern since they are used to providing a status.

Another antipattern typically seen in standups is that the team begins to solve problems as they become apparent. Standups are for realizing there are problems—not for solving them. Add the issues to a parking lot, and then create another meeting, which might be right after the standup, and solve problems there.

Teams run their own standups. When run well, standups can be very useful, provided the nature of the team's work requires intense collaboration. Make a conscious decision about when the team needs, or can effectively use, standups.

TIP ▶ *Encourage any team member to facilitate the standup instead of a project manager or leader to ensure it does not turn into a status meeting, but instead is used as a time for the team to self-organize and make commitments to each other.*

5.2.5 DEMONSTRATIONS/REVIEWS

As the team completes the features usually in the form of user stories, the team periodically demonstrates the working product. The product owner sees the demonstration and accepts or declines stories.

In iteration-based agile, the team demonstrates all completed work items at the end of the iteration. In flow-based agile, the team demonstrates completed work when it is time to do so, usually when enough features have accumulated into a set that is coherent. Teams, including the product owner, need feedback to decide how early to ask for product feedback.

As a general guideline, demonstrate whatever the team has as a working product at least once every 2 weeks. That frequency is enough for most teams, so team members can get feedback that prevents them from heading in a wrong direction. That is also frequent enough so that the teams can keep the product development clean enough to build a complete product as often as they want or need to.

A fundamental part of what makes a project agile is the frequent delivery of a working product. A team that does not demonstrate or release cannot learn fast enough and is likely not adopting agile techniques. The team may require additional coaching to enable frequent delivery.

5.2.6 PLANNING FOR ITERATION-BASED AGILE

Each team's capacity is different. Each product owner's typical story size is different. Teams consider their story size so they do not try to commit to more stories than there is team capacity to complete within one iteration.

When people are unavailable (e.g., holidays, vacations, or anything that prevents people from participating in the next set of work), the product owner understands that the team has reduced capacity. The team will not be able to finish the same amount of work as it finished in the previous time period. When teams have a reduced capacity, they will only plan for work that meets that capacity.

Teams estimate what they can complete, which is a measure of capacity (see Section 4.10 for examples). Teams cannot predict with 100% certainty what they can deliver, as they cannot know the unexpected. When product owners make the stories smaller and teams see progress in the form of a finished product, teams learn what they are able to do for the future.

Agile teams do not plan just once in one single chunk. Instead, agile teams plan a little, deliver, learn, and then replan a little more in an ongoing cycle.

 TIP

Draw the team's attention to the antipattern and help the team to discover how to improve its standups.

5.2.7 EXECUTION PRACTICES THAT HELP TEAMS DELIVER VALUE

If the team does not pay attention to quality, it will soon become impossible to release anything rapidly.

The following technical practices, many of which come from eXtreme Programming, may help the team to deliver at their maximum speed:

◆ **Continuous integration.** Perform frequent incorporation of work into the whole, no matter the product, and then retest to determine that the entire product still works as intended.

◆ **Test at all levels.** Employ system-level testing for end-to-end information and unit testing for the building blocks. In between, understand if there is a need for integration testing and where. Teams find smoke testing helpful as a first look at whether the work product is any good. Teams have found that deciding when to run regression tests and which ones helps them maintain product quality with good build performance. Agile teams have a strong preference for automated tests so they can build and maintain a momentum of delivery.

◆ **Acceptance Test-Driven Development (ATDD).** In ATDD, the entire team gets together and discusses the acceptance criteria for a work product. Then the team creates the tests, which allows the team to write just enough code and automated tests to meet the criteria. For non-software projects, consider how to test the work as the team completes chunks of value.

◆ **Test-Driven Development (TDD) and Behavior-Driven Development (BDD).** Writing automated tests before writing/creating the product actually helps people design and mistake-proof the product. For non-software projects, consider how to "test-drive" the team's designs. Hardware and mechanical projects often use simulations for interim tests of their designs.

◆ **Spikes (timeboxed research or experiments).** Spikes are useful for learning and may be used in circumstances such as: estimation, acceptance criteria definition, and understanding the flow of a user's action through the product. Spikes are helpful when the team needs to learn some critical technical or functional element.

5.2.8 HOW ITERATIONS AND INCREMENTS HELP DELIVER WORKING PRODUCT

Iterations help a team create a cadence for delivery and many kinds of feedback. Teams produce increments of value for delivery and feedback. The first part of this delivery is a demonstration. Teams receive feedback about how the product looks and operates through a demo. Team members retrospect to see how they can inspect and adapt their process to succeed.

Demonstrations or reviews are a necessary part of the agile project flow. Schedule the demonstration as appropriate for the team's delivery cadence.

5.3 TROUBLESHOOTING AGILE PROJECT CHALLENGES

Agile approaches were born out of the need to solve issues associated with high rates of change, uncertainty, and complexity on projects. Due to these origins, they contain a variety of tools and techniques for dealing with issues that present problems in predictive approaches. Refer to Table 5-1.

Teams should demo often for feedback and to show progress. Encourage the PMO and other interested parties to watch demonstrations so the people deciding on the project portfolio can see the actual progress.

Table 5-1. Agile Pain Points and Troubleshooting Possibilities

Pain Point	Troubleshooting Possibilities
Unclear purpose or mission for the team	Agile chartering for purpose—vision, mission, and mission tests
Unclear working agreements for the team	Agile chartering for alignment—values, principles, and working agreements
Unclear team context	Agile chartering for context—boundaries, committed assets, and prospective analysis
Unclear requirements	Help sponsors and stakeholders craft a product vision. Consider building a product roadmap using specification by example, user story mapping, and impact mapping. Bring the team and product owner together to clarify the expectations and value of a requirement. Progressively decompose roadmap into backlog of smaller, concrete requirements.
Poor user experience	User experience design practices included in the development team involve users early and often.
Inaccurate estimation	Reduce story size by splitting stories. Use relative estimation with the entire team to estimate. Consider agile modeling or spiking to understand what the story is.
Unclear work assignments or work progress	Help the team learn that they self-manage their work. Consider kanban boards to see the flow of work. Consider a daily standup to walk the board and see what work is where.
Team struggles with obstacles	A servant leader can help clear these obstacles. If the team doesn't know the options they have, consider a coach. Sometimes, the team needs to escalate stories the team or servant leader has not been able to remove.
Work delays/overruns due to insufficiently refined product backlog items	Product owner and team workshop stories together. Create a definition of ready for the stories. Consider splitting stories to use smaller stories.
Defects	Consider the technical practices that work for the environment. Some possibilities are: pair work, collective product ownership, pervasive testing (test-driven and automated testing approaches) and a robust definition of done.
Work is not complete	Team defines definition of done for stories including acceptance criteria. Also add release criteria for projects.
Technical debt (degraded code quality)	Refactoring, agile modeling, pervasive testing, automated code quality analysis, definition of done

Table 5-1. Agile Pain Points and Troubleshooting Possibilities *(cont.)*

Pain Point	Troubleshooting Possibilities
Too much product complexity	For software and non-software encourage the team always to be thinking "What is the simplest thing that would work?" and apply the agile principle of "Simplicity--the art of maximizing the amount of work not done". These help reduce complexity.
Slow or no improvement in the teamwork process	Capture no more than three items to improve at each retrospective. Ask the servant leader to help the team learn how to integrate those items.
Too much upfront work leading to rework	Instead of much upfront work, consider team spikes to learn. In addition, measure the WIP during the beginning of the project and see what the team's options are to deliver value instead of designs. Shorten iterations and create a robust definition of done.
False starts, wasted efforts	Ask the product owner to become an integral part of the team.
Inefficiently ordered product backlog items	Rank with value including cost of delay divided by duration (CD3) and other value models
Rush/wait uneven flow of work	Plan to the team's capacity and not more. Ask people to stop multitasking and be dedicated to one team. Ask the team to work as pairs, a swarm, or mob to even out the capabilities across the entire team.
Impossible stakeholder demands	Servant leadership to work with this stakeholder (and possibly product owner).
Unexpected or unforeseen delays	Ask the team to check in more often, use kanban boards to see the flow of work and work in progress limits to understand the impact of the demands on the team or product. Also track impediments and impediment removal on an impediment board.
Siloed teams, instead of cross-functional teams	Ask the people who are part of projects to self-organize as cross-functional teams. Use servant leadership skills to help the managers understand why agile needs cross-functional teams.

5.4 MEASUREMENTS IN AGILE PROJECTS

Transitioning to agile means using different measurements. Using agile means looking at new metrics that matter to the team and to management. These metrics matter because they focus on customer value.

One problem with status reporting is the team's ability to predict completion or to use traffic light status to describe the project. For instance, project leaders describe the project as "90% done." At that point the team tries to integrate the pieces into a product. The team discovers missing requirements or surprises, or finds that the product doesn't integrate the way they thought it would.

The project is only partway done, and the traffic light status reporting does not reflect the real state. Too often, the project team realizes it will need just as much time to complete the remainder of the project. For too many projects, the team realizes they are—at most—10% done because of issues the team discovered.

The problem with predictive measurements is that they often do not reflect reality. It often happens that a project status light is green up until 1 month before the release date; this is sometimes referred to as a watermelon project (green on the outside, red on the inside). Oftentimes project status lights turn red with seemingly no warnings, because there is no empirical data about the project until 1 month before the release date.

Metrics for agile projects contain meaningful information that provide a historical track record, because agile projects deliver value (finished work) on a regular basis. Project teams can use such data for improved forecasts and decision making.

Surrogate measurements such as percent done are less useful than empirical measurements such as finished features. See Section 4.10 for more information on value management. Agile helps teams see problems and issues so the team can diagnose and address them.

In addition to quantitative measures, the team can consider collecting qualitative measures. Some of these qualitative measures focus on practices the team has chosen and assess how well the team uses those practices, for example, the business satisfaction with delivered features, the morale of the team; and anything else the team wants to track as a qualitative measure.

5.4.1 AGILE TEAMS MEASURE RESULTS

Agile favors empirical and value-based measurements instead of predictive measurements. Agile measures what the team delivers, not what the team predicts it will deliver.

A team that is accustomed to having project baselines and estimates of earned value and ROI might be puzzled about working on a project and not managing to a baseline. Agile is based on working products of demonstrable value to customers.

Baselines are often an artifact of attempted prediction. In agile, the team limits its estimation to the next few weeks at most. In agile, if there is low variability in the team's work and if the team members are not multitasking, the team's capacity can become stable. This allows better prediction for the next couple of weeks.

After the team completes work in iteration or flow, the team can replan. Agile does not create the ability to do more work. However, there is evidence that the smaller the chunk of work, the more likely people are to deliver it.

Software product development, like other knowledge work, is about learning—learning while delivering value. Hardware development and mechanical development are similar in the design parts of the project. Learning takes place by experimenting, delivering small increments of value, and getting feedback on what has been accomplished thus far. Many other product development projects incorporate learning also.

Sponsors usually want to know when the project will be done. Once the team establishes a reliable velocity (average stories or story points per iteration) or the average cycle time, the team can predict how much longer the project will take.

As an example, if the team averages 50 story points per iteration, and the team estimates there are about another 500 points remaining, the team estimates it has about 10 iterations remaining. As the product owner refines the stories remaining and as the team refines its estimates, the project estimate could go up or down, but the team can provide an estimate.

If the team averages a cycle time of three days per story and there are 30 remaining stories, the team would have 90 business days remaining, approximately 4 to 5 months.

Reflect the estimate variability with hurricane-style charts, or some other variability measure that the sponsors will understand.

Because learning is such a large part of the project, the team needs to balance uncertainty and provide value to the customers. The team plans the next small part of the project. The team reports empirical data and replans further small increments to manage the project uncertainty.

Some iteration-based projects use burndown charts to see where the project is going over time. Figure 5-1 shows an example of a burndown chart where the team planned to deliver 37 story points. Story points rate the relative work, risk, and complexity of a requirement or story. Many agile teams use story points to estimate effort. The dotted burndown line is the plan. In Figure 5-1, the team can see by Day 3 that they are at risk for that delivery.

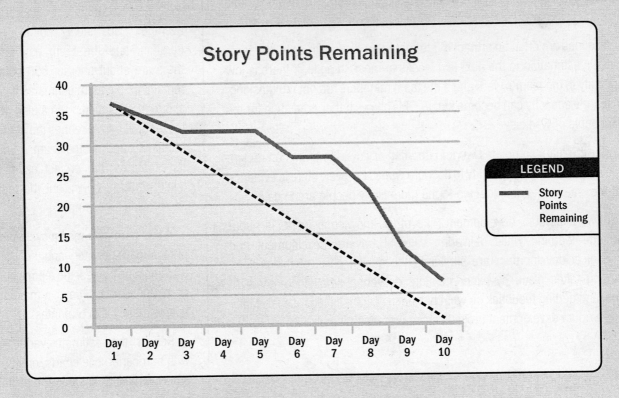

Figure 5-1. Burndown Chart for Remaining Story Points

Some project teams prefer burnup charts. The same data used in Figure 5-1 is shown in Figure 5-2 in a burnup chart.

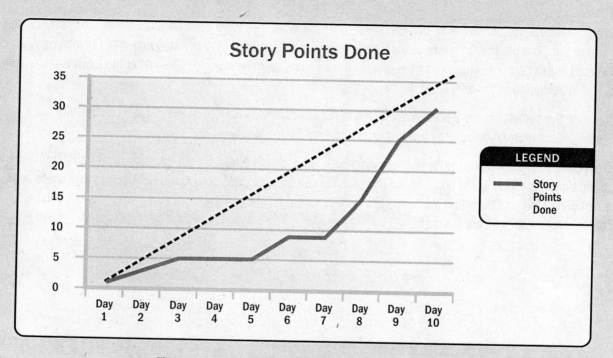

Figure 5-2. Burnup Chart for Showing Story Points Completed

Burnup charts show the work completed. The two charts in Figures 5-1 and 5-2 are based on the same data, but displayed in two different ways. Teams may prefer how to see their data.

When a team sees what it has not yet completed as it works through an iteration, the team may become dispirited and possibly rush to complete the work without meeting the acceptance criteria. However, the team could have any number of good reasons for not completing work as it expected. Burndowns show the effect of team members multitasking, stories that are too large, or team members out of the office.

Especially with teams new to agile, the burnup will show changes in scope during the iteration. Burnups allow teams to see what they have accomplished, which helps the team proceed to the next piece of work.

Whether teams use burndown or burnup charts, they see what they have completed as the iteration progresses. At the end of the iteration, they might base their next measure of capacity (how many stories or story points) on what they completed in this iteration. That allows the product owner along with the team to replan what the team is more likely to succeed in delivering in the next iteration.

Velocity, the sum of the story point sizes for the features actually completed in this iteration, allows the team to plan its next capacity more accurately by looking at its historical performance.

Flow-based agile teams use different measurements: lead time (the total time it takes to deliver an item, measured from the time it is added to the board to the moment it is completed), cycle time (the time required to process an item), and response time (the time that an item waits until work starts). Teams measure cycle time to see bottlenecks and delays, not necessarily inside the team.

TIP

Teams might discover it can take four to eight iterations to achieve a stable velocity. The teams need the feedback from each iteration to learn about how they work and how to improve.

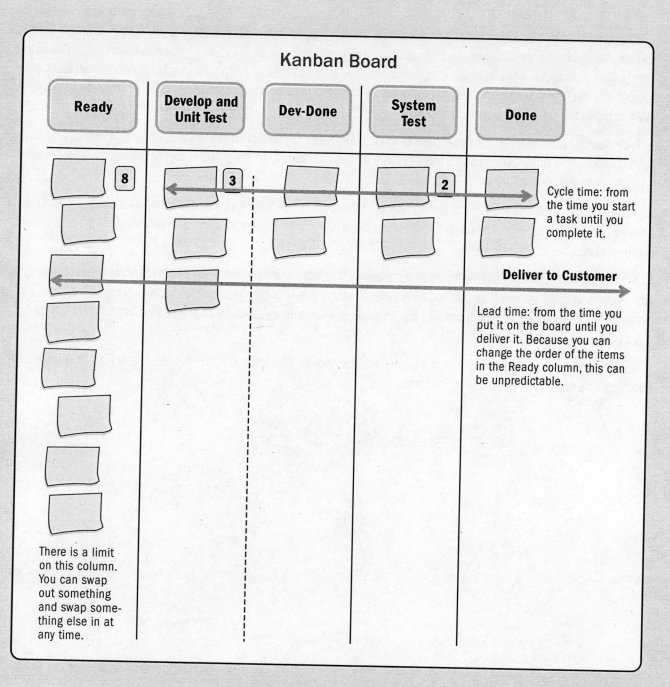

Figure 5-3. Example of a Kanban Board

Lead time is useful to understand cycle time from the first look at a particular feature to the length of time it took to release it to the customer. The work in progress (WIP) limits at the top of each column, shown in boxes here, allows the team to see how to pull work across the board. When the team has met its WIP limits, the team cannot pull work from the left into the next column. Instead, the team works from the right-most full column and asks, "What do we do as a team to move this work into the next column?"

Each feature is unique, so its cycle time is unique. However, a product owner might notice that smaller features have smaller cycle times. The product owner wants to see throughput, so the product owner creates smaller features or works with the team to do so.

Burnups, burndowns (capacity measures) and lead time, and cycle time (predictability measures) are useful for in-the-moment measurements. They help a team understand how much more work they have and whether the team might finish on time.

Measuring story points is not the same as measuring completed stories or features. Some teams attempt to measure story points without completing the actual feature or story. When teams measure only story points, they measure capacity, not finished work, which violates the principle of "the primary measure of progress is working software" (or, other product if not software).

Each team has its own capacity. When a team uses story points, be aware that the number of story points a team can complete in a given time is unique to that team.

TIP ►
When teams depend on external people or groups, measure cycle time to see how long it takes for the team to complete the work. Measure lead time to see the external dependencies after the team completes its work. Teams can also measure the reaction time, the time from ready to the first column, to see how long it takes them—on average—to respond to new requests.

When teams provide their own units of measure, teams are better able to assess and estimate and deliver their work. The downside of relative estimation is that there is no way to compare teams or add velocity across teams.

The team can measure completed work in a feature burnup/burndown chart and in a product backlog burnup chart. These charts provide trends of completion over time, as shown in Figure 5-4.

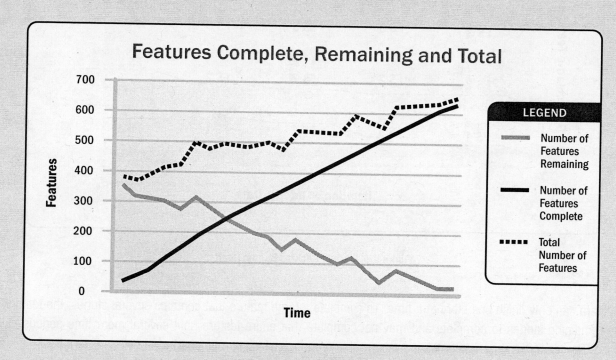

Figure 5-4. Feature Chart

Feature burnup/burndown charts may show that requirements grew during the project. The features complete line shows that the team completes features at a regular pace. The total features line shows how the project's total features changed over time. The features remaining burndown line shows that the rate of feature completion varies. Every time features are added to the project, the burndown line changes.

Earned value in agile is based on finished features, as shown in Figure 5-5. The product backlog burnup chart shows completed work compared to total expected work at interval milestones or iterations.

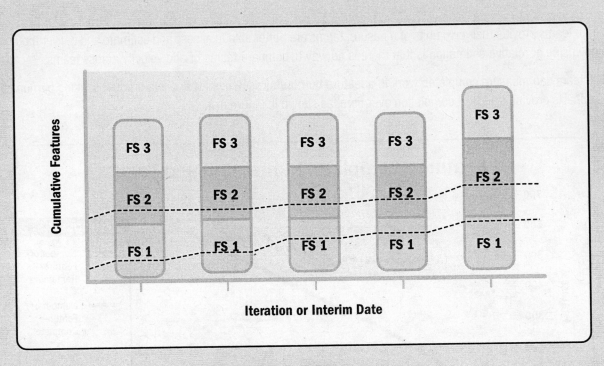

Figure 5-5. Product Backlog Burnup Chart

A team can only finish one story at a time. To complete a large feature that contains several stories, the team will have remaining stories to complete and may not complete that entire feature until several more time periods have passed. The team can show its completed value with a product backlog burnup chart as shown in Figure 5-5.

If a team needs to measure earned value, it can consider using this burnup chart in Figure 5-6 as an example: Note that the left Y axis represents story points as scope, and the right Y axis represents the project spend.

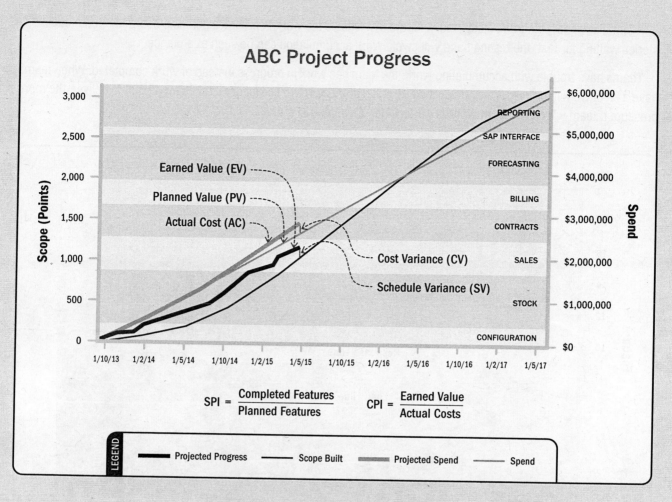

ABC Project Progress

SPI = $\dfrac{\text{Completed Features}}{\text{Planned Features}}$ CPI = $\dfrac{\text{Earned Value}}{\text{Actual Costs}}$

LEGEND
Projected Progress — Scope Built — Projected Spend — Spend

Figure 5-6. Earned Value in an Agile Context

Traditional EVM metrics like schedule performance index (SPI) and cost performance index (CPI) can be easily translated into agile terms. For example, if the team planned to complete 30 story points in an iteration, but only completed 25 then the SPI is 25/30 or 0.83 (the team is working at only 83% of the rate planned). Likewise, CPI is the earned value (completed features value) to date divided by the actual costs to date or, as shown in Figure 5-6, $2.2M / $2.8M = 0.79. This means a result of only 79 cents on the dollar compared to plan (but of course this assumes that the prediction is still correct.)

A cumulative flow diagram, illustrated in Figure 5-7, shows the work in progress across a board. If a team has many stories waiting for test, the testing band will swell. Work accumulation can be seen at a glance.

Teams have trouble with accumulating work: the team has work in progress instead of work completed. When teams have a lot of work in progress, they delay their overall feature delivery. The longer it takes for a team to deliver, the more pressure a team will have for yet more features in the same period of time.

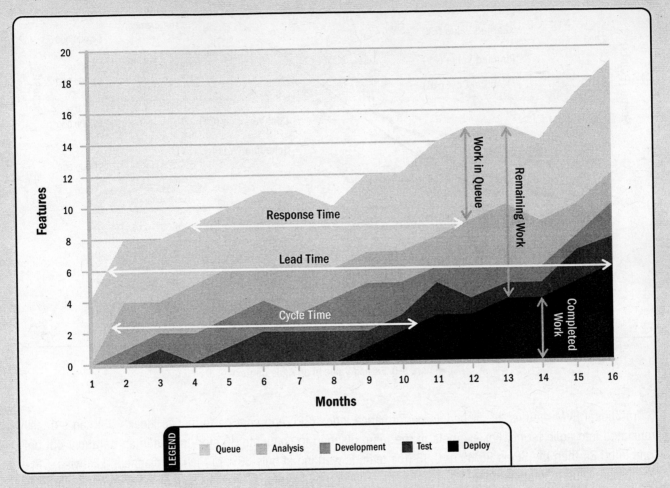

Figure 5-7. Cumulative Flow Diagram of Completed Features

Adapt this cumulative flow to the project task board.

6

ORGANIZATIONAL CONSIDERATIONS FOR PROJECT AGILITY

Every project exists in an organizational context. Cultures, structures, and policies can influence both the direction and the outcome of any project. These dynamics can challenge project leaders.

While project leaders may not have the ability to change organizational dynamics as they see fit, they are expected to navigate those dynamics skillfully.

This section explores the way the organization and in some circumstances, the project context, influences projects. Leaders can explore options for change, to increase project success.

> Project agility is more effective and sustained as the organization adjusts to support it.

6.1 ORGANIZATIONAL CHANGE MANAGEMENT

Organizational change management covers the skills and techniques for influencing changes that support agility.

The PMI publication, *Managing Change in Organizations: A Practice Guide* [2], describes a comprehensive and holistic approach for successfully introducing meaningful change. The recommendations offered there include:

◆ Models for describing change dynamics,

◆ Framework for achieving change, and

◆ Application of change management practices at the project, program, and portfolio levels.

Sections 6.1.1 and 6.1.2 explore the considerations of change management specific to an agile context.

Figure 6-1 shows the relationship between these two topics.

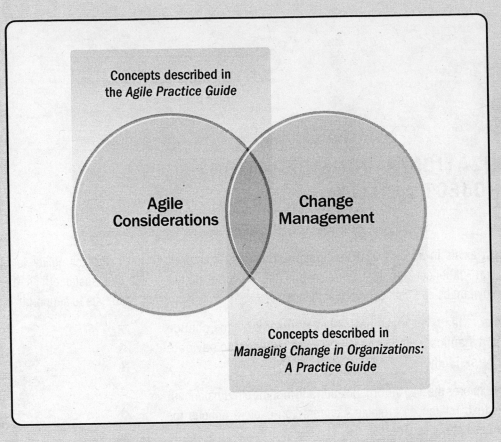

Figure 6-1. The Relationship Between Change Management and Agile Approaches

6.1.1 DRIVERS FOR CHANGE MANAGEMENT

All projects are about change. However, there are two key factors that further motivate the use of change management practices in an agile context:

◆ **Changes associated with accelerated delivery.** Agile approaches emphasize delivering project outputs early and often. However, the receiving organization may not be fully prepared to incorporate those outputs at an increased pace. Accelerating delivery will test the organization's ability to accommodate that delivery. Successfully discovering and delivering a project's features is not enough. If the organization resists the project's output, then the targeted return on investment is delayed. Customer acceptance of and alignment with project outputs becomes even more prevalent in an agile environment.

◆ **Changes associated with agile approaches.** Organizations just beginning to use agile approaches also experience high degrees of change. Higher degrees of collaboration may require more frequent handoffs between teams, departments, or vendors. Decomposing work into iterative prototypes involves rework that could be viewed negatively. Leaders should consider change management techniques to address the hurdles of transitioning to the use of agile approaches.

6.1.2 READINESS FOR CHANGE

Organizations beginning to use agile approaches should understand the relative compatibility of those methods with their current approaches. Some organizations will have characteristics that more easily support agile principles of cross-department collaboration, continuous learning, and evolving internal processes. Examples of these change-friendly characteristics include:

◆ Executive management's willingness to change;

◆ Organization's willingness to shift the way it views, reviews, and assesses employees;

◆ Centralization or decentralization of project, program, and portfolio management functions;

◆ Focus on short-term budgeting and metrics versus long-term goals; and

◆ Talent management maturity and capabilities.

Conversely, there are other institutional characteristics that may be roadblocks to achieving the changes associated with organizational agility. Examples of these include:

◆ Work is decomposed into departmental silos, creating dependencies that prevent accelerated delivery instead of building cross-functional teams with guidance from centers of competencies.

◆ Procurement strategies are based on short-term pricing strategies, rather than long-term competencies.

◆ Leaders are rewarded for local efficiencies rather than end-to-end flow of project delivery or optimizing the whole (in regard to the organization).

◆ Employees are specialized contributors with limited tools or incentives to diversify their skills instead of building T-shaped specialists.

◆ Decentralized portfolios pull employees simultaneously onto too many projects at once instead of keeping them focused on one project at a time.

The degree to which an organization is willing to review and modify these practices will determine how quickly and effectively agile approaches can be adopted. However, in response to these organizational impediments to agility, project leaders can try various approaches to accelerate a cultural compatibility for:

◆ Visible and active executive sponsorship,

◆ Change management practices, including communication and coaching,

◆ Progressively pacing the adoption of agile practices on a project-by-project basis

◆ Incremental introduction of agile practices to the team; and

◆ Leading by example by using agile techniques and practices where possible.

6.2 ORGANIZATIONAL CULTURE

An organization's culture is its DNA—its core identity. Culture will always influence the use of agile approaches. Organizational culture runs along a continuum, from highly predictive plans to lean startup where everything is an experiment. Although agile approaches fit well with the lean startup culture, a highly predictive organization can encourage empirical measurements, small experiments, and learning so they can move toward agility.

6.2.1 CREATING AN ENVIRONMENT OF SAFETY

Organizational culture is difficult to change, but the most important cultural norm in an organization willing to try any new method or technique is enabling a safe work environment.

Only in a safe, honest, and transparent environment can team members and leaders truly reflect on their successes to ensure their projects continue to advance, or apply lessons learned on failed projects so they do not fall back into the same patterns.

6.2.2 ASSESSING CULTURE

Every project finds itself in tension with competing aspirations. How can the team go fast without compromising quality? How can the team preserve flexibility while also hitting a firm date? Most importantly, how does the team satisfy and meet the requirements of the customer?

Project leaders may feel their job is to meet every expectation of every stakeholder; but, when compelled to make a choice, there is often a priority depending on the culture and requirements of the organization's business environment. For example, a mobile telecom project has a greater bias for speed, where a government program may have a greater bias for generalization and stability.

> "Culture eats strategy for breakfast" —Peter Drucker
>
> This statement stresses the importance of people's commitment and passion for a cause. No matter what strategy or plan you implement with your team, its success is going to be governed by the people implementing the plan. If the people who are driving the strategy aren't passionate about the change, or worse, are apathetic about their job and their organization, then you stand little chance of implementing the change.

To navigate these dynamics, project leaders should take the time to assess where emphasis is most often applied in the organization. Figure 6-2 illustrates what an assessment might look like. In this example, a project leader initiates a conversation about organizational priorities with stakeholders, team members, and senior management. Those priorities are then recorded as positions on a sliding scale between two extremes. The results are then used to find agile techniques that best fit with those priorities.

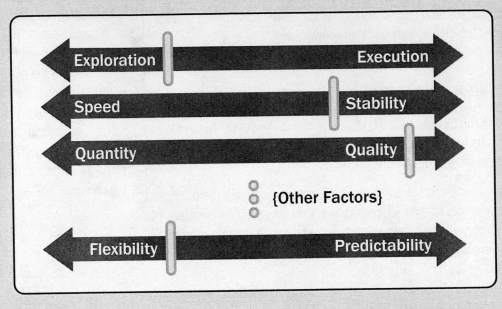

Figure 6-2. Example of Assessing Organizational Culture

Several models exist for assessing such dynamics; however, the model or method used is not that important. It is more critical that project leaders invest the effort to understand the forces that shape their context. Understanding the organization and the industry requirements that an organization needs to satisfy allows for choosing the right conversations, the right tradeoffs, and, especially, the right techniques.

6.3 PROCUREMENT AND CONTRACTS

As mentioned earlier in this practice guide, the Agile Manifesto values "customer collaboration over contract negotiation." Many project failures stem from breakdowns in the customer–supplier relationship. Projects incur more risk when those involved in the contract take the perspective of winners vs. losers. A collaborative approach is one that pursues a shared-risk-reward relationship, where all sides win. Some contracting techniques that can formalize this dynamic include the following:

◆ **Multi-tiered structure.** Rather than formalizing an entire contracting relationship in a single document, project parties can achieve more flexibility by describing different aspects in different documents. Mostly fixed items (e.g., warranties, arbitration) can be locked in a master agreement. Meanwhile, all parties list other items subject to change (e.g., services rates, product descriptions) in a schedule of services. The contract can reference them in the master services agreement. Finally, more dynamic items such as scope, schedule, and budget can be formalized in a lightweight statement of work. Isolating the more changing elements of a contract into a single document simplifies modifications and thus flexibility.

◆ **Emphasize value delivered.** Many vendor relationships are governed by fixed milestones or "phase gates" focused on intermediate artifacts, rather than a full deliverable of incremental business value. Often, these controls limit the use of feedback to improve the product. Instead, milestones and payment terms can be structured based on value-driven deliverables in order to enhance the project's agility.

◆ **Fixed-price increments.** Rather than lock an entire project scope and budget into a single agreement, a project can decompose the scope into fixed-price microdeliverables, such as user stories. For the customer, this gives more control over how the money is spent. For the supplier, it limits the financial risk of over-commitment to a single feature or deliverable.

◆ **Not-to-exceed time and materials.** Customers incur unwanted risk from a traditional time and materials approach. One alternative is to limit the overall budget to a fixed amount. This allows the customer to incorporate new ideas and innovations into the project not originally planned. When customers want to incorporate new ideas, they will have to manage to a given capacity, replacing original work with new work. Work should be closely monitored as hours allocated reach their limit. Also, additional contingency hours could be planned into the maximum budget if considered helpful.

◆ **Graduated time and materials.** Another alternative is a shared financial risk approach. In agile, the quality criteria are part of what done means. Therefore, the supplier can be rewarded with a higher hourly rate when delivery is earlier than the contracted deadline. Conversely, the supplier would suffer a rate reduction for late delivery.

◆ **Early cancellation option.** When an agile supplier delivers sufficient value with only half of the scope completed, the customer should not be bound to pay the remaining half if the customer no longer needs it. Instead, a contract can offer the customer to buy the remainder of the project for a cancellation fee. The customer limits budget exposure and the supplier earns positive revenue for services no longer required.

◆ **Dynamic scope option.** For those contracts with a fixed budget, a supplier may offer the customer the option to vary the project scope at specified points in the project. The customer can adjust features to fit the capacity. Then the customer can leverage innovation opportunities, while limiting the supplier's risk of over commitment.

◆ **Team augmentation.** Arguably the most collaborative contracting approach is to embed the supplier's services directly into the customer organization. Funding teams instead of a specific scope preserves the customer's strategic discretion on what work should actually be done.

◆ **Favor full-service suppliers.** In order to diversify risk, customers may seek a multisupplier strategy. However, the temptation will be to contract the work such that each supplier does only one thing, which creates a web of dependencies before any usable service or product emerges. Instead, place an emphasis on engagements that deliver full value (as in the idea of completed independent feature sets).

It is possible to create agile contracts. Agile is built on a synergy of collaboration and trust. The supplier can help by delivering value early and often. The customer can help by providing timely feedback.

6.4 BUSINESS PRACTICES

The willingness and ability to create new competences within an organization when the need arises is a mark of organizational agility. These do not have to be earth-shattering changes and could be less disruptive in an organization that is focused on agility and the results it provides. Transparency and open collaboration are absolutely key.

As cross-functional teams deliver value, the teams and individuals might encounter problems with various support functions in the organization.

As team delivers value on a regular basis, finance departments may have the opportunity to capitalize the product differently. If the team has contracts with other organizations, procurement departments may need to change those contracts to help the other organizations deliver value frequently and synchronize with the team.

Once teams start to work in a cohesive and cooperative manner, they will challenge internal management policies. Human resources may notice individual incentives make less sense, and managers may struggle with the performance appraisals of self-organizing employees. In each case, these are opportunities to review the degree to which existing practices support agile ways of working.

As organizations progress to greater agility, there will be obvious needs for additional business units to change the way they interact and perform their responsibilities. The changes that have benefited other areas of the organization should now be embraced so the effectiveness of the entire organization can be realized.

6.5 MULTITEAM COORDINATION AND DEPENDENCIES (SCALING)

Many projects incur dependencies, even when they are not managed within a given program. For this reason, it is necessary to have an understanding of how agile works within an existing program and portfolio management context.

6.5.1 FRAMEWORKS

The guidance of the most widespread agile methods such as Scrum and eXtreme Programming focus on the activities of a single, small, usually colocated, cross-functional team. While this is very useful for efforts that require a single team, it may provide insufficient guidance for initiatives that require the collaboration of multiple agile teams in a program or portfolio.

A range of frameworks (such as the Scaled Agile Framework, Large Scale Scrum, and Disciplined Agile) and approaches (e.g., Scrum of Scrums) have emerged to cater to just such circumstances. More details on these can be found in Annex A3.

6.5.2 CONSIDERATIONS

There is more than one way to scale work. The team might need to scale the work of several agile projects into a single agile program. Alternatively, the organization can design a structure that supports agile approaches across the entire portfolio.

For example, it is helpful to start small and learn as rapidly as possible what works well in the organizational context. Teams can achieve successful outcomes even when everything is not completely transformed into an agile approach.

Regardless of the approach, a critical success factor is the healthy agile team. If using an agile approach for a single team is not successful, do not try to scale up to using it more broadly; instead, address the organizational impediments that prevent teams from working in an agile way.

The goal of large-scale agile projects is to coordinate the efforts of different teams to bring value to customers. There is more than one way to do that. Teams may use a formal framework or apply agile thinking to adjust existing program management practices.

6.6 AGILE AND THE PROJECT MANAGEMENT OFFICE (PMO)

The PMO exists to shepherd business value throughout the organization. It might do this by helping projects achieve their goals. Sometimes, the PMO educates teams (or arranges for training) and supports projects. Sometimes, the PMO advises management about the relative business value for a given project or set of projects.

Because agile creates cultural change, over time, the organization might need to change, including the PMO. For example, managers make decisions about which projects to fund and when, and teams decide what they need for training or advice.

6.6.1 AN AGILE PMO IS VALUE-DRIVEN

Any project should deliver the right value, to the right audience, at the right time. The PMO's objective is to facilitate and enable this goal. An agile-based PMO approach is based on a customer-collaboration mindset and is present in all PMO programs. In many cases, this means the PMO operates as if it were a consulting business, tailoring its efforts to meet specific needs requested by a given project. Some projects may need tools and templates, while others may benefit from executive coaching. The PMO should strive to deliver what is needed and keep the pulse on its customers to ensure that it knows and is able to adapt to their needs. This intrapreneur approach focuses on the PMO activities that are perceived as the most valuable to the projects it supports.

6.6.2 AN AGILE PMO IS INVITATION-ORIENTED

In order to accelerate progress on a value-based charter, a PMO may be tempted to mandate certain solutions or approaches, for example, to make everyone do it the same way to get some quick wins. However, a more deliberate perspective incorporates the desire for employee engagement. This is achieved by inviting only those interested to engage with PMO services. Higher engagement with PMO practices makes it easier for those practices to be "sticky." If the PMO is delivering value to its clients, it is more likely that clients will request its services and adopt its practices.

6.6.3 AN AGILE PMO IS MULTIDISCIPLINARY

In order to support project-specific needs, the PMO needs to be conversant in several competencies beyond project management itself, because different projects require distinct capabilities. For instance, one project may need organizational design to address staffing challenges while another may require organizational change management techniques for stakeholder engagement or unique business models to support customer goals.

Some organizations have been transforming their PMOs into agile centers of excellence that provide such services as:

◆ **Developing and implementing standards.** Provide templates for user stories, test cases, cumulative flow diagrams, etc. Provide agile tools and educate supporting groups on iterative development concepts.

◆ **Developing personnel through training and mentoring.** Coordinate agile training courses, coaches, and mentors to help people transition to an agile mindset and upgrade their skills. Encourage and support people to attend local agile events.

◆ **Multiproject management.** Coordinate between agile teams by communicating between projects. Consider sharing items such as progress, issues, and retrospective findings and improvement experiments. Help manage major customer releases at the program level and investment themes at the portfolio level using an appropriate framework.

◆ **Facilitating organizational learning.** Gather project velocity profiles and capture, store, and index retrospective findings.

◆ **Managing stakeholders.** Provide product owner training, guidance on acceptance testing, and how to evaluate and give feedback on systems. Champion the importance of subject matter experts (SMEs) to projects.

◆ **Recruiting, selecting, and evaluating team leaders.** Develop guidelines for interviewing agile practitioners.

◆ **Executing specialized tasks for projects.** Train and provide retrospective facilitators, create agreements with agile project troubleshooters, and provide mentors and coaches.

6.7 ORGANIZATIONAL STRUCTURE

The structure of an organization strongly influences its ability to pivot to new information or shifting market needs. Here is a listing of key characteristics:

◆ **Geography.** Geographically distributed and dispersed project organizations may find several challenges impeding their work on any project. Project leaders and regional managers may have alternative or even competing goals. Additionally, cultural differences, language barriers, and lower visibility can slow down productivity. Fortunately, the use of agile approaches can encourage more collaboration and confidence than would otherwise exist. Project leaders in these contexts should encourage dialog at the team and executive level to tailor techniques for the context and to manage expectations about the effort required to do so.

◆ **Functionalized structures.** Some organizations are structured on a spectrum ranging from highly projectized to matrixed to highly functionalized. Projects with highly functionalized structures may find general resistance to collaboration across its organization.

◆ **Size of project deliverable.** Reducing the size of a project deliverable will motivate more frequent handoffs across departments, and thus more frequent interactions and a faster flow of value across the organization.

◆ **Allocation of people to projects.** Another approach is to ask for a single person from each department to be temporarily, yet fully allocated, to the highest priority project.

◆ **Procurement-heavy organizations.** Some organizations choose to implement projects primarily through vendors. Although project goals may be clear, vendors have a responsibility to look after their own financial viability. Moreover, once vendors complete their obligations and leave the engagement, the associated project knowledge goes with them. This limits the internal competencies needed for sustained flexibility and speed. Agile techniques such as retrospectives and follow up on possible improvement areas when the vendor is still engaged can help mitigate loss of product knowledge.

6.8 EVOLVING THE ORGANIZATION

When addressing an individual challenge area or implementing a new hybrid or agile approach, it is recommended to undertake the work incrementally. A common practice is to treat the change process as an agile project with its own backlog of changes that could be introduced and prioritized by the team, based on perceived value or other considerations. Each of the changes can be treated as an experiment, which is tested for a short period of time to determine suitability as-is or the need for further refinement/consideration.

Use kanban boards to track progress, showing the new approaches already in use as "done," those being tried as "in progress," and those still waiting to be introduced as "to do." See Figure 6-3 for the initial board with a ranked backlog. Figure 6-4 shows an example of what a board might have as work progresses.

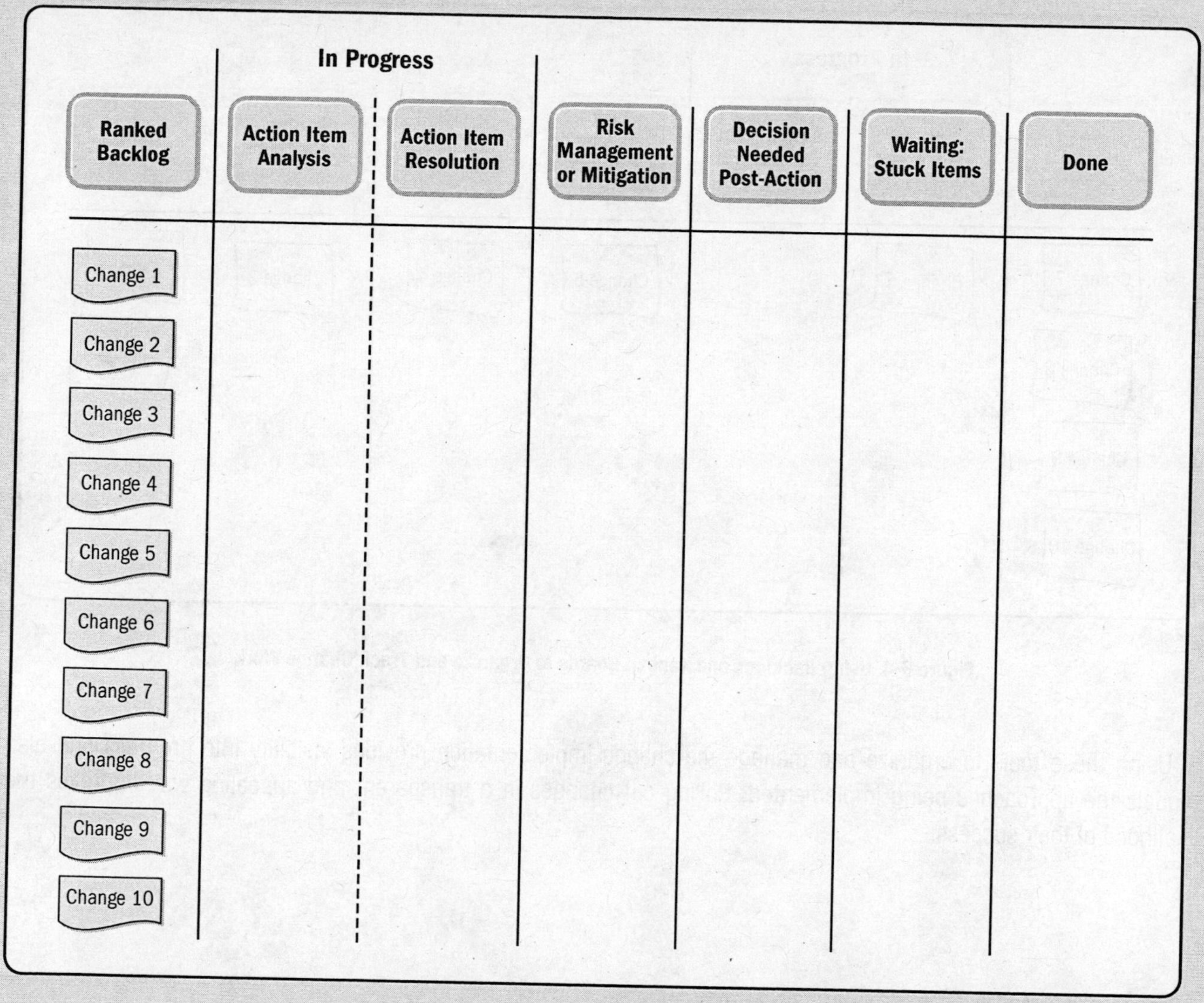

Ranked Backlog	In Progress		Risk Management or Mitigation	Decision Needed Post-Action	Waiting: Stuck Items	Done
	Action Item Analysis	Action Item Resolution				
Change 1						
Change 2						
Change 3						
Change 4						
Change 5						
Change 6						
Change 7						
Change 8						
Change 9						
Change 10						

Figure 6-3. Initial Ranked Backlog for Changes

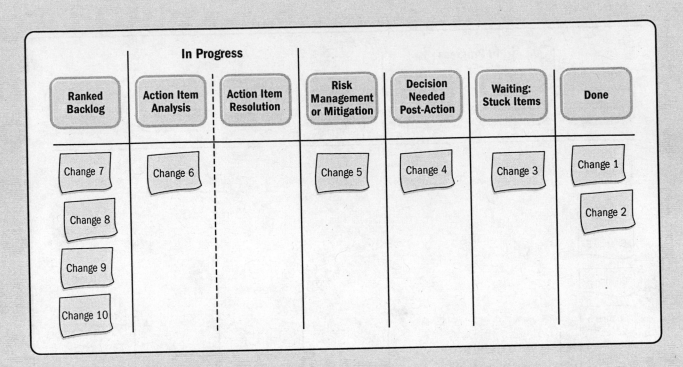

Figure 6-4. Using Backlogs and Kanban Boards to Organize and Track Change Work

Using these tools to organize and manage the change implementation provides visibility into progress and also models the approaches being implemented. Rolling out changes in a transparent and appealing way improves the likelihood of their success.

7

A CALL TO ACTION

The adoption of agile and its approaches for managing projects has increased dramatically since the Agile Manifesto was first published in 2001. Adoption and the desire to operate with an agile mindset is no longer limited to a certain sized organization or those specializing only in information technology. The mindset applies universally and the approaches are successful in many settings.

Today, the demand for "being agile" is higher than ever. The debate over the best path to agility continues to keep the conversation and innovation evolving. One truth remains constant—inspection, adaptation, and transparency are critical to successfully delivering value.

You may not see everything you expected to see in this practice guide. Our core team realizes you may disagree with some elements or approaches we did choose to present—and passionately so. We call on your passion to continue the conversation and improve the next iteration of this practice guide. This is your journey—learn, experiment, gain feedback, and experiment again. Then help us retrospect; give us feedback on the guidance and contribute to future editions of this practice guide. After all, inspection without adaptation is wasted effort.

Lastly, we want to encourage you to be engaged in the broader communities of project management and agile to further conversations on these topics. Look for representatives from both PMI and Agile Alliance® at conferences and meetings and engage them in discussion. Use social media and blog your thoughts and opinions.

You can provide feedback and engage in conversation regarding the contents of this practice guide at the blog called "Agile in Practice" at https://www.projectmanagement.com/blogs/347350/Agile-in-Practice.

ANNEX A1
PMBOK® GUIDE MAPPING

Table A1-1 illustrates the mapping of Project Management Process Groups to the Knowledge Areas defined in the *PMBOK® Guide* – Sixth Edition.

This annex describes how hybrid and agile approaches address the attributes described in the *PMBOK® Guide* Knowledge Areas (see Table A1-2). It covers what stays the same and what may be different along with some guidelines to consider for increasing the likelihood of success.

Table A1-1. Project Management Process Group and Knowledge Area Mapping

Knowledge Areas	Project Management Process Groups				
	Initiating Process Group	Planning Process Group	Executing Process Group	Monitoring and Controlling Process Group	Closing Process Group
4. Project Integration Management	4.1 Develop Project Charter	4.2 Develop Project Management Plan	4.3 Direct and Manage Project Work 4.4 Manage Project Knowledge	4.5 Monitor and Control Project Work 4.6 Perform Integrated Change Control	4.7 Close Project or Phase
5. Project Scope Management		5.1 Plan Scope Management 5.2 Collect Requirements 5.3 Define Scope 5.4 Create WBS		5.5 Validate Scope 5.6 Control Scope	
6. Project Schedule Management		6.1 Plan Schedule Management 6.2 Define Activities 6.3 Sequence Activities 6.4 Estimate Activity Durations 6.5 Develop Schedule		6.6 Control Schedule	
7. Project Cost Management		7.1 Plan Cost Management 7.2 Estimate Costs 7.3 Determine Budget		7.4 Control Costs	
8. Project Quality Management		8.1 Plan Quality Management	8.2 Manage Quality	8.3 Control Quality	
9. Project Resource Management		9.1 Plan Resource Management 9.2 Estimate Activity Resources	9.3 Acquire Resources 9.4 Develop Team 9.5 Manage Team	9.6 Control Resources	
10. Project Communications Management		10.1 Plan Communications Management	10.2 Manage Communications	10.3 Monitor Communications	
11. Project Risk Management		11.1 Plan Risk Management 11.2 Identify Risks 11.3 Perform Qualitative Risk Analysis 11.4 Perform Quantitative Risk Analysis 11.5 Plan Risk Responses	11.6 Implement Risk Responses	11.7 Monitor Risks	
12. Project Procurement Management		12.1 Plan Procurement Management	12.2 Conduct Procurements	12.3 Control Procurements	
13. Project Stakeholder Management	13.1 Identify Stakeholders	13.2 Plan Stakeholder Engagement	13.3 Manage Stakeholder Engagement	13.4 Monitor Stakeholder Engagement	

Table A1-2. Application of Agile in *PMBOK® Guide* Knowledge Areas

PMBOK® Guide Knowledge Area	Application in an Agile Work Process
Section 4 **Project Integration Management**	Iterative and agile approaches promote the engagement of team members as local domain experts in integration management. The team members determine how plans and components should integrate. The expectations of the project manager as noted in the *Key Concepts for Integration Management* sections in the *PMBOK® Guide* do not change in an adaptive environment, but control of the detailed product planning and delivery is delegated to the team. The project manager's focus is on building a collaborative decision-making environment and ensuring the team has the ability to respond to changes. This collaborative approach can be further enhanced when team members possess a broad skill base rather than a narrow specialization.
Section 5 **Project Scope Management**	In projects with evolving requirements, high risk, or significant uncertainty, the scope is often not understood at the beginning of the project or it evolves during the project. Agile methods deliberately spend less time trying to define and agree on scope in the early stage of the project and spend more time establishing the process for its ongoing discovery and refinement. Many environments with emerging requirements find that there is often a gap between the real business requirements and the business requirements that were originally stated. Therefore, agile methods purposefully build and review prototypes and release versions in order to refine the requirements. As a result, scope is defined and redefined throughout the project. In agile approaches, the requirements constitute the backlog.

PMBOK® Guide Knowledge Area	Application in an Agile Work Process
Section 6 **Project Schedule Management**	Adaptive approaches use short cycles to undertake work, review the results, and adapt as necessary. These cycles provide rapid feedback on the approaches and suitability of deliverables, and generally manifest as iterative scheduling and on-demand, pull-based scheduling, as discussed in the Key Trends and Emerging Practices section for Project Schedule Management in the *PMBOK® Guide*. In large organizations, there may be a mixture of small projects and large initiatives requiring long-term roadmaps to manage the development of these programs using scaling factors (e.g., team size, geographical distribution, regulatory compliance, organizational complexity, and technical complexity). To address the full delivery life cycle for larger, enterprise-wide systems, a range of techniques utilizing a predictive approach, adaptive approach, or a hybrid of both, may need to be adopted. The organization may need to combine practices from several core methods, or adopt a method that has already done so, and adopt a few principles and practices of more traditional techniques. The role of the project manager does not change based on managing projects using a predictive development life cycle or managing projects in adaptive environments. However, to be successful in using adaptive approaches, the project manager will need to be familiar with the tools and techniques to understand how to apply them effectively.
Section 7 **Project Cost Management**	Projects with high degrees of uncertainty or those where the scope is not yet fully defined may not benefit from detailed cost calculations due to frequent changes. Instead, lightweight estimation methods can be used to generate a fast, high-level forecast of project labor costs, which can then be easily adjusted as changes arise. Detailed estimates are reserved for short-term planning horizons in a just-in-time fashion. In cases where high-variability projects are also subject to strict budgets, the scope and schedule are more often adjusted to stay within cost constraints.

Table A1-2. Application of Agile in *PMBOK® Guide* Knowledge Areas *(cont.)*

PMBOK® Guide Knowledge Area	Application in an Agile Work Process
Section 8 **Project Quality Management**	In order to navigate changes, agile methods call for frequent quality and review steps built in throughout the project rather than toward the end of the project. Recurring retrospectives regularly check on the effectiveness of the quality processes. They look for the root cause of issues then suggest trials of new approaches to improve quality. Subsequent retrospectives evaluate any trial processes to determine if they are working and should be continued or new adjusting or should be dropped from use. In order to facilitate frequent, incremental delivery, agile methods focus on small batches of work, incorporating as many elements of project deliverables as possible. Small batch systems aim to uncover inconsistencies and quality issues earlier in the project life cycle when the overall costs of change are lower.
Section 9 **Project Resource Management**	Projects with high variability benefit from team structures that maximize focus and collaboration, such as self-organizing teams with generalizing specialists. Collaboration is intended to boost productivity and facilitate innovative problem solving. Collaborative teams may facilitate accelerated integration of distinct work activities, improve communication, increase knowledge sharing, and provide flexibility of work assignments in addition to other advantages. Although the benefits of collaboration also apply to other project environments, collaborative teams are often critical to the success of projects with a high degree of variability and rapid changes, because there is less time for centralized tasking and decision making. Planning for physical and human resources is much less predictable in projects with high variability. In these environments, agreements for fast supply and lean methods are critical to controlling costs and achieving the schedule.

PMBOK® Guide Knowledge Area	Application in an Agile Work Process
Section 10 **Project Communications Management**	Project environments subject to various elements of ambiguity and change have an inherent need to communicate evolving and emerging details more frequently and quickly. This motivates streamlining team member access to information, frequent team checkpoints, and colocating team members as much as possible. In addition, posting project artifacts in a transparent fashion, and holding regular stakeholder reviews are intended to promote communication with management and stakeholders.
Section 11 **Project Risk Management**	High-variability environments, by definition, incur more uncertainty and risk. To address this, projects managed using adaptive approaches make use of frequent reviews of incremental work products and cross-functional project teams to accelerate knowledge sharing and ensure that risk is understood and managed. Risk is considered when selecting the content of each iteration, and risks will also be identified, analyzed, and managed during each iteration. Additionally, the requirements are kept as a living document that is updated regularly, and work may be reprioritized as the project progresses, based on an improved understanding of current risk exposure.

Table A1-2. Application of Agile in *PMBOK® Guide* Knowledge Areas *(cont.)*

PMBOK® Guide Knowledge Area	Application in an Agile Work Process
Section 12 **Project Procurement Management**	In agile environments, specific sellers may be used to extend the team. This collaborative working relationship can lead to a shared risk procurement model where both the buyer and the seller share in the risk and rewards associated with a project. Larger projects may use an adaptive approach for some deliverables and a more stable approach for other parts. In these cases, a governing agreement such as a master services agreement (MSA) may be used for the overall engagement, with the adaptive work being placed in an appendix or supplement. This allows changes to occur on the adaptive scope without impacting the overall contract.
Section 13 **Project Stakeholder Management**	Projects experiencing a high degree of change require active engagement and participation with project stakeholders. To facilitate timely, productive discussion and decision making, adaptive teams engage with stakeholders directly rather than going through layers of management. Often the client, user, and developer exchange information in a dynamic co-creative process that leads to more stakeholder involvement and higher satisfaction. Regular interactions with the stakeholder community throughout the project mitigate risk, build trust, and support adjustments earlier in the project cycle, thus reducing costs and increasing the likelihood of success for the project. In order to accelerate the sharing of information within and across the organization, agile methods promote aggressive transparency. The intent of inviting any stakeholders to project meetings and reviews or posting project artifacts in public spaces is to surface as quickly as possible any misalignment, dependency, or other issue related to the changing project.

ANNEX A2
AGILE MANIFESTO MAPPING

This annex describes how the elements of the Agile Manifesto are covered in the *Agile Practice Guide*.

Table A2-1. Agile Manifesto Values Covered in the *Agile Practice Guide*

Value	*Agile Practice Guide* Coverage by Section and Title
Individuals and interactions over processes and tools	4.2 Servant Leadership Empowers the Team 4.3 Team Composition 5.1 Charter the Project and the Team 5.2.4 Daily Standups 6.2 Organizational Culture
Working software over comprehensive documentation	5.2.2 Backlog Preparation 5.2.3 Backlog Refinement 5.2.5 Demonstrations/Reviews 5.2.7 Execution Practices that Help Teams Deliver Value
Customer collaboration over contract negotiation	4.3 Team Composition 5.4 Measurements in Agile Projects 6.2 Organizational Culture 6.3 Procurement and Contracts 6.7 Organizational Structure
Responding to change over following a plan	5.2.1 Retrospectives 5.2.3 Backlog Refinement 5.2.5 Demonstrations/Reviews

Table A2-2. *Agile Practice Guide* **Mapping of Principles Behind the Agile Manifesto**

Principle	Agile Practice Guide Coverage
Our highest priority is to satisfy the customer through early and continuous delivery of valuable software.	3.1 Characteristics of Project Life Cycles 5.2.7 Execution Practices that Help Teams Deliver Value
Welcome changing requirements, even late in development. Agile processes harness change for the customer's competitive advantage.	5.2.3 Backlog Refinement
Deliver working software frequently, from a couple of weeks to a couple of months, with a preference to the shorter timescale.	5.2 Common Agile Practices
Business people and developers must work together daily throughout the project.	4.2 Servant Leadership Empowers the Team 5.2.2 Backlog Preparation 5.2.3 Backlog Refinement
Build projects around motivated individuals. Give them the environment and support they need, and trust them to get the job done.	4.3 Team Composition 5.1 Charter the Project and the Team 5.2.1 Retrospectives
The most efficient and effective method of conveying information to and within a development team is face-to-face conversation.	4.3.4 Team Structures 5.2.4 Daily Standups
Working software is the primary measure of progress.	5.2.7 Execution Practices that Help Teams Deliver Value 5.2.8 How Iterations and Increments Help Delivery Working Product
Agile processes promote sustainable development. The sponsors, developers, and users should be able to maintain a constant pace indefinitely.	5.1 Charter the Project and the Team
Continuous attention to technical excellence and good design enhances agility.	5.2 Common Agile Practices
Simplicity—the art of maximizing the amount of work not done is essential.	5.2.2 Backlog Preparation 5.2.3 Backlog Refinement
The best architectures, requirements, and designs emerge from self-organizing teams.	4.3 Team Composition
At regular intervals, the team reflects on how to become more effective, then tunes and adjusts its behavior accordingly.	5.2.1 Retrospectives

ANNEX A3
OVERVIEW OF AGILE AND LEAN FRAMEWORKS

This annex describes some of the commonly used agile approaches. These approaches can be used as is or combined to adapt to what works best for a given environment or situation. It is not necessary to use any of these; an agile approach can be developed from scratch as long as it adheres to the mindset, values, and principles of the Agile Manifesto. If the agile principles are followed to deliver value at a sustainable pace, and the developed approach promotes collaboration with the customer, a specific approach is not required. A link to more information regarding each approach can be found in the Bibliography section of this guide.

A3.1 SELECTION CRITERIA FOR THE *AGILE PRACTICE GUIDE*

There are too many agile approaches and techniques to be explicitly included in this practice guide. Figure A3-1 depicts a sample of agile approaches based on their depth of guidance and breadth of their life cycles. The specific approaches selected for discussion are popular examples that are:

◆ **Designed for holistic use.** Some agile approaches are centered on a single project activity, such as estimation or reflecting. The listed examples include only the more holistic agile frameworks. Some are more full-featured than others, but all of the selected approaches are those intended to guide a broad set of project activities.

◆ **Formalized for common use.** Some agile frameworks are proprietary in nature and designed for specific use by a single organization or within a single context. The frameworks described in Sections A3.2 through A3.14 focus on those intended for common use in a variety of contexts.

◆ **Popular in modern use.** Some agile frameworks are holistically designed and well formalized, but are simply not commonly being used in most projects or organizations. The agile frameworks described in this annex have been adopted by a significant number of industries, as measured by a collection of recent industry surveys.

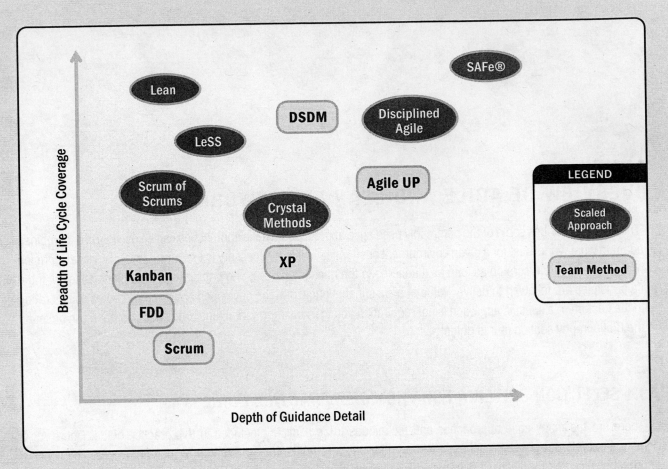

Figure A3-1. Agile Approaches Plotted by Breadth and Detail

A3.2 SCRUM

Scrum is a single-team process framework used to manage product development. The framework consists of Scrum roles, events, artifacts, and rules, and uses an iterative approach to deliver working product. Scrum is run on timeboxes of 1 month or less with consistent durations called sprints where a potentially releasable increment of product is produced. Table A3-1 lists Scrum events and artifacts utilized for project execution.

The Scrum team consists of a product owner, development team, and scrum master.

◆ The product owner is responsible for maximizing the value of the product.

◆ The development team is a cross-functional, self-organizing team consisting of team members who have everything they need within the team to deliver working product without depending on others outside of the team.

◆ The scrum master is responsible for ensuring the Scrum process is upheld and works to ensure the Scrum team adheres to the practices and rules as well as coaches the team on removing impediments.

Table A3-1. Scrum Events and Artifacts

Events	Artifacts
Sprint	Product backlog
Sprint planning	Sprint backlog
Daily scrum	Increments
Sprint review	
Sprint retrospective	

A3.3 EXTREME PROGRAMMING

eXtreme Programming (XP) is a software development method based on frequent cycles. The name is based on the philosophy of distilling a given best practice to its purest, simplest form, and applying that practice continuously throughout the project.

XP is most known for popularizing a holistic set of practices intended to improve the results of software projects. The method was first formalized as a set of twelve primary practices, but then gradually evolved to adopt several other corollary practices. These are listed in Table A3-2.

Table A3-2. The Practices of eXtreme Programming

XP Practice Area	Primary	Secondary
Organizational	• Sit together • Whole team • Informative workspace	• Real customer involvement • Team continuity • Sustainable pace
Technical	• Pair programming • Test-first programming • Incremental design	• Shared code/collective ownership • Documentation from code and tests • Refactoring
Planning	• User stories • Weekly cycle • Quarterly cycle • Slack	• Root cause analysis • Shrinking teams • Pay per use • Negotiated scope contract • Daily standups
Integration	• 10-minute build • Continuous integration • Test-first	• Single code base • Incremental deployment • Daily deployment

This evolution was the result of designing and adopting techniques through the filter of core values (communication, simplicity, feedback, courage, respect), and informed by key principles (humanity, economics, mutual benefit, self-similarity, improvement, diversity, reflection, flow, opportunity, redundancy, failure, quality, baby steps, accepted responsibility).

A3.4 KANBAN METHOD

Kanban in lean manufacturing is a system for scheduling inventory control and replenishment. This process of "just-in-time" inventory replenishment was originally seen in grocery stores when shelves were restocked based on the gaps in the shelves and not supplier inventory. Inspired by these just-in-time inventory systems, Taiichi Ohno developed Kanban and it was applied at the main Toyota manufacturing facility in 1953.

The word *kanban* is literally translated as "visual sign" or "card." Physical kanban boards with cards enable and promote the visualization and flow of the work through the system for everyone to see. This information radiator (large display) is made up of columns that represent the states the work needs to flow through in order to get to done. The simplest of boards could have three columns (i.e., to do, doing, and done), but it is adaptable to whatever states are deemed needed by the team utilizing it.

The Kanban Method is utilized and applicable in many settings and allows for a continuous flow of work and value to the customer. The Kanban Method is less prescriptive than some agile approaches and thus less disruptive to begin implementing as it is the original "start where you are" method. Organizations can begin applying Kanban Methods with relative ease and progress toward fully implementing the method if that is what they deem necessary or appropriate.

Unlike most agile approaches, the Kanban Method does not prescribe the use of timeboxed iterations. Iterations can be used within the Kanban Method, but the principle of pulling single items through the process continuously and limiting work in progress to optimize flow should always remain intact. The Kanban Method may be best used when a team or organization is in need of the following conditions:

◆ **Flexibility.** Teams are typically not bound by timeboxes and will work on the highest priority item in the backlog of work.

◆ **Focus on continuous delivery.** Teams are focused on flowing work through the system to completion and not beginning new work until work in progress is completed.

◆ **Increased productivity and quality.** Productivity and quality are increased by limiting work in progress.

◆ **Increased efficiency.** Checking each task for value adding or non-value-added activities and removing the non-value adding activities.

◆ **Team member focus.** Limited work in progress allows the team to focus on the current work.

◆ **Variability in the workload.** When there is unpredictability in the way that work arrives, and it becomes impossible for teams to make predictable commitments; even for short periods of time.

◆ **Reduction of waste.** Transparency makes waste visible so it can be removed.

The Kanban Method is derived from lean thinking principles. The defining principles and the core properties of the Kanban Method are listed in Table A3-3.

The Kanban Method is a holistic framework for incremental, evolutionary process and systems change for organizations. The method uses a "pull system" to move the work through the process. When the team completes an item, the team can pull an item into that step.

Table A3-3. Defining Principles and Properties of the Kanban Method

Defining Principles	Core Properties
Start with current state	Visualize the workflow
Agree to pursue incremental, evolutionary change	Limit work in progress
Respect the current process, roles, responsibilities, and titles	Manage flow
	Make process policies explicit
Encourage acts of leadership at all levels	Implement feedback loops
	Improve collaboratively

Kanban boards, such as the one shown in Figure A3-2, are a low-tech, high-touch technology that may seem overly simplistic at first, but those using them soon realize their power. Utilizing policies for entry and exit to columns, as well as constraints such as limiting work in process, kanban boards provide clear insight to workflow, bottlenecks, blockers, and overall status. Additionally the board acts as an information radiator to anyone who sees it, providing up-to-date information on the status of the work of the team.

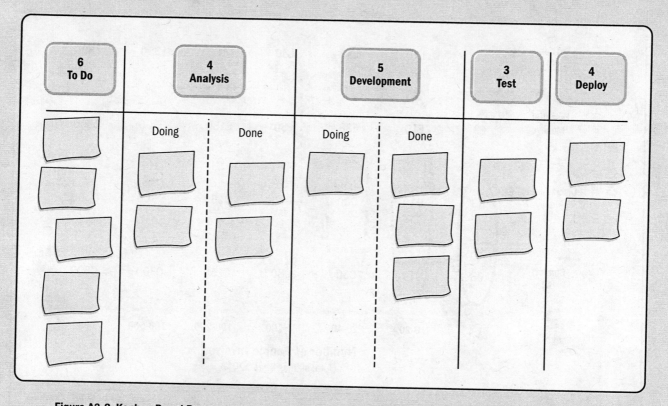

Figure A3-2. Kanban Board Demonstrating Work in Progress Limits, and a Pull System to Optimize the Flow of Work

In the Kanban Method, it is more important to complete work than it is to start new work. There is no value derived from work that is not completed so the team works together to implement and adhere to the work in progress (WIP) limits and get each piece of work through the system to "done."

A3.5 CRYSTAL METHODS

Crystal is a family of methodologies. Crystal methodologies are designed to scale, and provide a selection of methodology rigor based on project size (number of people involved in the project) and the criticality of the project.

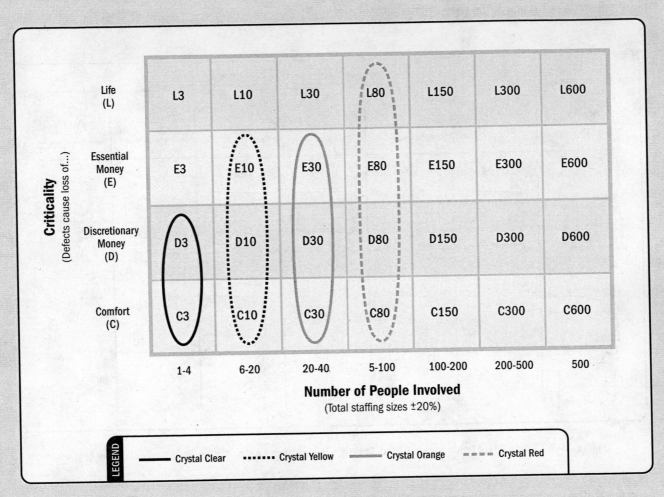

Figure A3-3. The Crystal Family of Methods

Crystal Methodology realizes that each project may require a slightly tailored set of policies, practices, and processes in order to meet the project's unique characteristics. The family of methodologies use different colors based on "weight" to determine which methodology to use. The use of the word crystal comes from the gemstone where the various "faces" represent underlying core principles and values. The faces are a representation of techniques, tools, standards, and roles listed in Table A3-4.

Table A3-4. The Core Values and Common Properties of Crystal

Core Values	Common Properties[A]
People	Frequent delivery
Interaction	Reflective improvement
Community	Close or osmotic communication
Skills	Personal safety
Talents	Focus
Communications	Easy access to expert users
	Technical environment with automated tests, configuration management, and frequent integration

[A] The more these properties are in a project, the more likely it is to succeed.

A3.6 SCRUMBAN

Scrumban is an agile approach originally designed as a way to transition from Scrum to Kanban. As additional agile frameworks and methodologies emerged, it became an evolving hybrid framework in and of itself where teams use Scrum as a framework and Kanban for process improvement.

In Scrumban, the work is organized into small "sprints" and leverages the use of kanban boards to visualize and monitor the work. The stories are placed on the kanban board and the team manages its work by using work-in-progress limits. Daily meetings are held to maintain the collaboration between the team and to remove impediments. A planning trigger is set in place for the team to know when to plan next, typically when the work-in-progress level is lower than a predetermined limit. There are no predefined roles in Scrumban—the team retains their current roles.

A3.7 FEATURE-DRIVEN DEVELOPMENT

Feature-Driven Development (FDD) was developed to meet the specific needs of a large software development project. Features relate to a small business value capability.

There are six primary roles on a Feature-Driven Development project where individuals can take on one or more of the following roles:

◆ Project manager,

◆ Chief architect,

◆ Development manager,

◆ Chief programmer,

◆ Class owner, and/or

◆ Domain expert.

A Feature-Driven Development project is organized around five processes or activities, which are performed iteratively:

◆ Develop an overall model,

◆ Build a features list,

◆ Plan by feature,

◆ Design by feature, and

◆ Build by features.

The life cycle flow and interaction of these five processes is illustrated in Figure A3-4.

Feature-Driven Development activities are supported by a core set of software engineering best practices:

◆ Domain object modeling,

◆ Developing by feature,

◆ Individual class ownership,

◆ Feature teams,

◆ Inspections,

◆ Configuration management,

◆ Regular builds, and

◆ Visibility of progress and results.

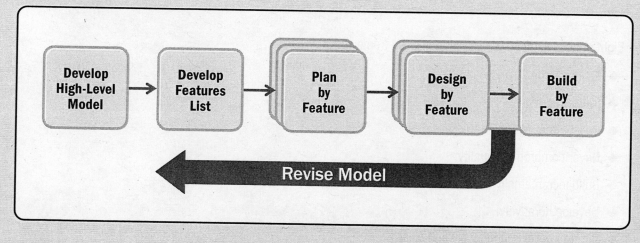

Figure A3-4. Feature-Driven Development Project Life Cycle

A3.8 DYNAMIC SYSTEMS DEVELOPMENT METHOD

Dynamic Systems Development Method (DSDM) is an agile project delivery framework initially designed to add more rigor to existing iterative methods popular in the 1990s. It was developed as a noncommercial collaboration among industry leaders.

DSDM is known best for its emphasis on constraint-driven delivery. The framework will set cost, quality, and time at the outset, and then use formalized prioritization of scope to meet those constraints as shown in Figure A3-5.

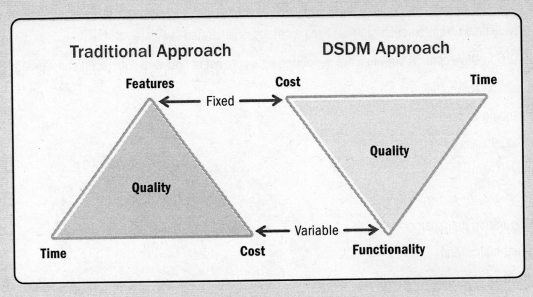

Figure A3-5. DSDM Approach to Constraint-Driven Agility

Eight principles guide the use of the DSDM framework:

- ◆ Focus on the business need.
- ◆ Deliver on time.
- ◆ Collaborate.
- ◆ Never compromise quality.
- ◆ Build incrementally from firm foundations.
- ◆ Develop iteratively.
- ◆ Communicate continuously and clearly.
- ◆ Demonstrate control (use appropriate techniques).

A3.9 AGILE UNIFIED PROCESS

The Agile Unified Process (AgileUP) is an offshoot of the Unified Process (UP) for software projects. It features more accelerated cycles and less heavyweight processes than its Unified Process predecessor. The intent is to perform more iterative cycles across seven key disciplines, and incorporate the associated feedback before formal delivery. The disciplines along with guiding principles are listed in Table A3-5.

Table A3-5. The Key Elements of the Agile Unified Process

Disciplines within a Release	Principles Guiding the Disciplines
Model	The team knows what it's doing
Implementation	Simplicity
Test	Agility
Deployment	Focus on high-value activities
Configuration management	Tool independence
Project management	Tailoring to fit
Environment	Situationally specific

A3.10 SCALING FRAMEWORKS

A3.10.1 SCRUM OF SCRUMS

Scrum of Scrums (SoS), also known as "meta Scrum," is a technique used when two or more Scrum teams consisting of three to nine members each need to coordinate their work instead of one large Scrum team. A representative from each team attends a meeting with the other team representative(s), potentially daily but typically two to three times a week. The daily meeting is conducted similar to the daily standup in Scrum where the representative reports completed work, next set of work, any current impediments, and potential upcoming impediments that might block the other team(s). The goal is to ensure the teams are coordinating work and removing impediments to optimize the efficiency of all the teams.

Large projects with several teams may result in conducting a Scrum of Scrum of Scrums, which follows the same pattern as SoS with a representative from each SoS reporting into a larger group of representatives as shown in Figure A3-6.

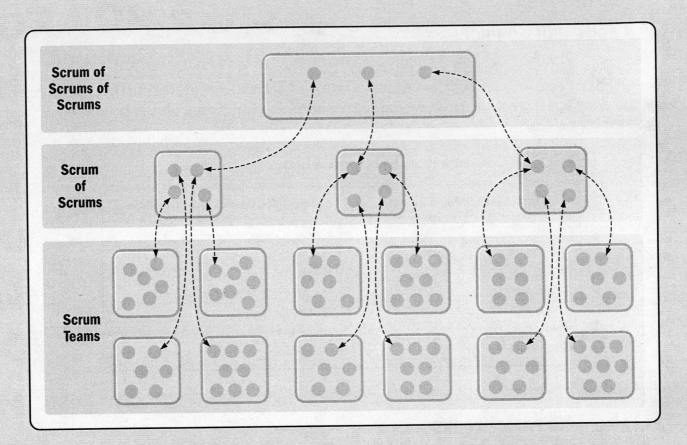

Figure A3-6. Representatives of Scrum Teams Participating in SoS teams

A3.11 SCALED AGILE FRAMEWORK

The Scaled Agile Framework (SAFe®) focuses on providing a knowledge base of patterns for scaling development work across all levels of the enterprise.

SAFe® is focused on the following principles:

◆ Take an economic view.

◆ Apply systems thinking.

◆ Assume variability; preserve options.

◆ Build incrementally with fast, integrated learning cycles.

◆ Base milestones on objective evaluation of working systems.

- Visualize and limit work in progress, reduce batch sizes, and manage queue lengths.

- Apply cadence; synchronize with cross-domain planning.

- Unlock the intrinsic motivation of knowledge workers.

- Decentralize decision making.

SAFe® focuses on detailing practices, roles, and activities at the portfolio, program, and team levels with an emphasis on organizing the enterprise around value streams that focus on providing continuous value to the customer.

A3.12 LARGE SCALE SCRUM (LeSS)

Large Scale Scrum (LeSS) is a framework for organizing several development teams toward a common goal extending the Scrum method shown in Figure A3-6. The core organizing principle is to retain as much as possible of the elements of the conventional single-team Scrum model. This helps minimize any extensions to the model that might create unnecessary confusion or complexity. Table A3-6 shows a comparison of LeSS and Scrum.

Table A3-6. Comparison of LeSS and Scrum

Similarities of LeSS and Scrum	LeSS Techniques Added to Scrum
One single product backlog	Sprint planning is more formally divided into two parts of what and how
One definition of done for all teams	
One potentially shippable product increment at the end of each sprint	Organic cross-team coordination
	Overall cross-team refinement
One product owner	Overall retrospective focused on cross-team improvements
Complete, cross-functional teams	
One sprint	

In order to extend Scrum without losing its essence, LeSS promotes the use of certain discerning principles, such as systems thinking, whole product focus, transparency, and others.

A3.13 ENTERPRISE SCRUM

Enterprise Scrum is a framework designed to apply the Scrum method on a more holistic organizational level rather than a single product development effort. Specifically, the framework advises organization leaders to:

◆ Extend the use of Scrum across all aspects of the organization;

◆ Generalize the Scrum techniques to apply easily at those various aspects; and

◆ Scale the Scrum method with supplemental techniques as necessary.

The intent is to use agile approaches beyond project execution by enabling disruptive innovation.

A3.14 DISCIPLINED AGILE (DA)

Disciplined Agile (DA) is a process decision framework that integrates several agile best practices into a comprehensive model. DA was designed to offer a balance between those popular methods deemed to be either too narrow in focus (e.g., Scrum) or too prescriptive in detail (e.g., AgileUP). To achieve that balance, it blends various agile techniques according to the following principles:

◆ **People-first.** Enumerating roles and organization elements at various levels.

◆ **Learning-oriented.** Encouraging collaborative improvement.

◆ **Full delivery life cycle.** Promoting several fit-for-purpose life cycles.

◆ **Goal-driven.** Tailoring processes to achieve specific outcomes.

◆ **Enterprise awareness.** Offering guidance on cross-departmental governance.

◆ **Scalable.** Covering multiple dimensions of program complexity.

APPENDIX X1
CONTRIBUTORS AND REVIEWERS

X1.1 *AGILE PRACTICE GUIDE* CORE COMMITTEE

The following individuals were members of the project Core Committee responsible for drafting the guide, including review and adjudication of reviewer recommendations.

X1.1.1 REPRESENTING THE PROJECT MANAGEMENT INSTITUTE:

Mike Griffiths, PMP, PMI-ACP, (Committee Chair)
Jesse Fewell, CST, PMI-ACP
Horia Slușanschi, PhD, CSM
Stephen Matola, BA, PMP

X1.1.2 REPRESENTING AGILE ALLIANCE:

Johanna Rothman, MS (Committee Vice Chair)
Becky Hartman, PMI-ACP, CSP
Betsy Kauffman, ICP-ACC, PMI-ACP

X1.2 *AGILE PRACTICE GUIDE* SUBJECT MATTER EXPERT REVIEWERS

The following individuals were invited subject matter experts who reviewed the draft and provided recommendations through the SME Review.

Joe Astolfi, PMP, PSM

Maria Cristina Barbero, PMI-ACP, PMP

Michel Biedermann, PhD, PMI-ACP

Zach Bonaker

Robert Bulger, PfMP, CSM

Sue Burk

Shika Carter, PMP, PMI-ACP

Lauren Clark, PMP, CSM

Linda M Cook, CSM, CSPO

Pamela Corbin-Jones, PMI-ACP, CSM

Jeff Covert

Alberto Dominguez, MSc, PMP

Scott P. Duncan, CSM, ICP-ACC

Sally Elatta, PMI-ACP, EBAC

Frank R. Hendriks, PMP, PMI-ACP

Derek Huether

Ron Jeffries

Fred Koos

Philippe B. Kruchten, PhD, PEng

Steve Mayner, SPCT4, PMP

Michael S. McCalla, PMI-ACP, CSP

Don B. McClure, PMP, PMI-ACP

Anthony C. Mersino, PMI-ACP, CSP

Kenneth E. Nidiffer, PhD, PMP

Michael C. Nollet, PMP, PMI-ACP

Laura Paton, MBA, PMP

Yvan Petit, PhD, PMP

Dwayne Phillips, PhD, PMP

Piyush Prakash, PMP, Prince2

Dave Prior, PMP, CST

Daniel Rawsthorne, PhD, PMP

Annette D. Reilly, PMP, PhD

Stephan Reindl, PMI-ACP, PMP

Reed D. Shell, PMP, CSP

Cindy Shelton, PMP, PMI-ACP

Teresa Short

Lisa K. Sieverts, PMP, PMI-ACP

Christopher M. Simonek, PMP, CSM

Robert "Sellers" Smith, PMP, PMI-ACP

Ram Srinivasan, PMP, CST

Chris Stevens, PhD

Karen Strichartz, PMP, PMI-ACP

Rahul Sudame, PMI-ACP

Joanna L. Vahlsing, PMP

Erik L. van Daalen

Annette Vendelbo, PMP, PMI-ACP

Dave Violette, MPM, PMP

Anton Vishnyak, PMI-ACP, CSM

Chuck Walrad, MA, MS

X1.3 FORMAT FOCUS GROUP

The following individuals assisting in the development of new content style and formatting elements for the *Agile Practice Guide*.

Goran Banjanin, PgMP, PMP
Andrew Craig
Cătălin-Teodor Dogaru, PhD, PMP
Jorge Espinoza, PMP
Jennifer M. Forrest, CSM, PMP
Helen Fotos, PMP, PMI-ACP
Dave Hatter, PMP, PMI-ACP
Christopher Healy, PMP
Mike Hoffmann, MBA, PMP
Chadi Kahwaji, PMP
Rajaraman Kannan, PMP, MACS CP
Amit Khanna PMP, PMI–ACP
Ariel Kirshbom, PMI-ACP, CSP
Bernardo Marques, PMP
Noura Saad, PMI-ACP, CSPO
Kurt Schuler, PMP
Demetrius L. Williams, MBA, PMP
Liza Wood
Melody Yale, CSP, SPC4

X1.4 PMI STANDARDS MEMBER ADVISORY GROUP (MAG)

The following individuals are members of the PMI Standards Member Advisory Group, who provided direction to and final approval on behalf of PMI for the *Agile Practice Guide*.

Maria Cristina Barbero, PMI-ACP, PMP
Brian Grafsgaard, PMP, PgMP
Hagit Landman, PMP, PMI-SP
Yvan Petit PhD, PMP
Chris Stevens, PhD
Dave Violette, MPM, PMP
John Zlockie, MBA, PMP, PMI Standards Manager

X1.5 AGILE ALLIANCE® BOARD

The following individuals are members of Agile Alliance Board of Directors, who provided direction to and final approval on behalf of Agile Alliance for the *Agile Practice Guide*.

Juan Banda
Phil Brock (Managing Director)
Linda Cook
Stephanie Davis
Ellen Grove
Paul Hammond (Chair)
Victor Hugo Germano
Rebecca Parsons (Secretary)
Craig Smith
Declan Whelan

X1.6 PMI SUPPORT STAFF AND ACADEMIC RESEARCH SUPPORT

The following individuals worked to support the core committee in the development and approval of the draft, in support of the Format Focus Group, and in PMI marketing efforts.

Melissa M. Abel, Marketing Communications Specialist
Karl F. Best, PMP, CStd, Standards Specialist
Alicia C. Burke, MBA, CSM, Product Manager, Credentials
Edivandro C. Conforto, PhD, PMI Consultant on Agile Research
Dave Garrett, CSPO, Vice President, Transformation
Erica Grenfell, Administrative Assistant to VP, Organization Relations
M. Elaine Lazar, MA, MA, AStd, Project Specialist
Andrew Levin, PMP, Project Manager
Tim E. Ogline, User Experience Designer
Stephen A. Townsend, Director of Network Programs
Michael Zarro, PhD, UX Researcher

X1.7 PMI PRODUCTION STAFF

Donn Greenberg, Manager, Publications
Kim Shinners, Publications Production Associate
Roberta Storer, Product Editor
Barbara Walsh, Production Supervisor

APPENDIX X2
ATTRIBUTES THAT INFLUENCE TAILORING

X2.1 INTRODUCTION

This appendix provides high-level guidance on when and how to tailor agile approaches. It can be used to determine circumstances that might warrant changing or introducing new techniques, and then offers some recommendations to consider.

X2.2 FIRST SOME CAUTIONS

Tailoring is an advanced topic that should be undertaken by experienced practitioners who have been successful using agile approaches as originally described in multiple environments before they consider tailoring them. In other words, gain experience and be successful with one approach before attempting to tailor the approach.

> The Shu-Ha-Ri model of skills acquisition describes progression from obeying the rules (Shu 守, means to obey and protect), through consciously moving away from the rules (Ha 破, means to change or digress), and finally through steady practice and improvement finding an individual path (Ri 離, means to separate or leave). We need to start and practice at the Shu level before we are ready to move to the Ha level to tailor the process or the Ri level to invent a new custom process.

A common response when struggling to adopt an agile practice is to consider whether to do it or not. A statement like "Retrospectives were unpopular so we decided to drop them" illustrates this issue and indicates a more fundamental problem on the team that is unlikely to be addressed by tailoring the method. The situation will be made worse by omitting the retrospective activity that aims to improve the process.

Finally, tailoring should be undertaken in collaboration with the teammates or whoever the change is likely to impact. People need to be engaged in the thinking and decision-making process about changing processes in order for them to commit and buy-in to the changes in order to have a successful transition. Omitting people from tailoring a process is likely to result in resistance and resentment to the change, even if it makes good sense technically. Often, experienced coaches or leaders can help to engage people effectively.

X2.3 HOW TO USE THIS APPENDIX

To benefit from the guidance listed in this appendix, we recommend first successfully using the agile approaches as designed. Then review the tailoring guidelines in Table X2-1 that match the situation and read the associated recommendations. Next, discuss the change with the people it will impact and agree on a course of action.

As discussed in Section 5, a good way to evaluate a change is try it for an iteration or two first before adopting it permanently. Or, consider a flow-based approach to try to deliver several features. Then, reflect with a retrospective and reassess.

When people know they can experiment and provide feedback on the experiment, they are more likely to try something new. Having tried it for a timeboxed period, the team should review its effectiveness at a retrospective to determine whether it should be continued as-is, modified to improve it, or dropped from use.

Finally, successfully adopted, tailored approaches can be institutionalized into the standard processes used for projects that share these characteristics. It is also recommended that guidelines from Section 5 be followed that describe adopting (or tailoring) new approaches.

X2.4 TAILORING RECOMMENDATIONS

Listed below are some good practices to consider before tailoring an approach.

X2.4.1 BEWARE OF TAKING THINGS AWAY

Many of the agile practices act as self-supporting pairs. For instance, colocation and frequent business conversations allow for lightweight requirements since gaps in understanding can be filled quickly. Likewise, XP's ruthless testing allows for courageous refactoring as one practice supports the other. Removing something without understanding or addressing its counterbalanced practice will likely create more problems than it solves.

X2.4.2 USE THE TAILORING GUIDELINES TABLE

Using Table X2-1, find the circumstances that match a given situation and consider recommendations for tailoring. Discuss any changes with those who will be impacted by the change and plan a short trial first, along with an honest follow-up review before committing to the change.

Table X2-1. Tailoring Guidelines

Situation	Tailoring Recommendation
Very large project teams	Restructure large projects as multiple smaller projects. Try a technology trial project first and then an implementation project.
	Consider more frequent releases of fewer features each, which allows for the creation of smaller project teams.
	Consider reducing the team down to its critical core members. Often too many people hinder a process, not help it. Reducing a team size can reduce churn as well as costs.
	Break large teams into multiple smaller teams and use program management to synchronize and coordinate.
	Use agile and lean program management to organize the larger effort.
	Consider a scaled agile or lean framework such as DA, SAFe®, or LeSS. Each offers some useful ideas, and each carries implementation risks and process weight/cost.

Situation	Tailoring Recommendation
Dispersed teams	Many projects have (some) dispersed team members. Tools like instant messaging, video conferencing, and electronic team boards help bridge many of the communication gaps.
	When teams are likely to remain stable, set up face-to-face meetings as soon as possible to make future remote conversations more effective. People who have met face-to-face are more likely to enter unfiltered debate because of higher trust.
	When conducting meetings with remote participants where there is a loss of facial and body-language cues, consider round-robin check-ins to ensure participation and check consensus for decisions.
	Also, consider the use of iteration-based agile approaches. When team members are many time zones apart, consider using whole-project interactions less frequently, while encouraging more personal meetings (two or three people at a time) more frequently.
Some safety critical products may require additional documentation and conformance checks beyond what agile processes suggest out-of-the-box	Agile approaches can still be used in these environments, but they need to have the appropriate additional layers of conformance review, documentation, and certification that is required by the domain. In that case, documentation could be part of what the team delivers along with finished features. Features may not be done until the documentation is completed.
	Consider using a hybrid approach (multiple agile approaches) to get the benefits of improved collaboration and communication brought by agile with the added rigor required by the product environment. Aircraft flight system developers and drug companies use agile approaches coupled with their own additional processes to leverage the benefits and retain appropriate controls.
Stable requirements and execution process	Is agile really needed? If uncertainty in requirements is low, low rates of change, or minimal execution risk, the full suite of agile approaches may not be needed. While any project benefits from increased collaboration and transparency; some of the iterative build and review cycles might be overkill.
	If build/feedback cycles do not routinely uncover or refine requirements, consider extending their durations to minimize the cost impact of review time.
	If the project has high rates of change during design and development, but rolling it out to customers is a defined and repeatable process, hybrid approaches that use the appropriate life cycle model for each project phase may make more sense.
Teams are in functional silos inside functional organizations	Agile is built on the idea of cross-functional teams. Consider asking people to create cross-functional teams themselves, without management involvement and see what happens.
	If the compensation system is organized to recognize and reward functional areas, consider changing that first. People might not act in the interest of the product or the team until it affects their compensation in some way.

Table X2-1. Tailoring Guidelines *(cont.)*

Situation	Tailoring Recommendation
Transparency can cause fear	Agile creates a culture of transparency: people show and share their work throughout development. This sharing of interim deliverables and being open and honest about successes, failures, and current state is transparency. Transparency requires courage. Lead by example and demonstrate transparency in decision-making processes by using a status board or whiteboard.
Many of the team members have little technical domain knowledge	Agile approaches encourage and make use of self-directing teams to make local decisions about work items, such as task sequencing and which approach to use when solving a problem. When the majority of team members are inexperienced, consensus-based approaches may lead to problems and rework. So, for these teams, additional help "assigning" and "directing" may be necessary until the team gains the necessary skills. In other words, do not just declare that agile will be used and let an inexperienced team try to figure everything out because they are empowered and self-directing. Consider building centers of competencies to help provide guidance and build domain knowledge.
Lack of executive buy-in	When executive buy-in is missing, teams will encounter a clash between the agile mindset and approaches and the more predictive mindset and approaches. Find common ground, areas for improvement based on the organization's needs, and then use experiments and retrospectives to progress. Consider education/training for executives. Consider explaining agile in terms of lean thinking: short cycles, small batch sizes, frequent reviews, and retrospectives with small improvements.
Agile terms and language do not fit the organizational culture	Modify the terms so people will understand and agree to the activities, if not the agile language. Be specific about what each term means. For example, if the organization finds the word "game" unprofessional, don't use terms such as "planning game." Instead, consider using the term "planning workshop."

APPENDIX X3
AGILE SUITABILITY FILTER TOOLS

X3.1 INTRODUCTION

Agile literature contains many agile suitability filter tools to help assess under what circumstances an agile approach is appropriate to use. In 1994, the Dynamic Systems Development Method (DSDM) developed an Agile Project Suitability Questionnaire and an Organizational Suitability Questionnaire to help gauge likely fit and potential problem areas.

The Crystal family of approaches also employed suitability criteria, ranking projects by team size and the criticality of the product or service being developed. Crystal recommends that smaller, less critical projects be undertaken with lighter controls and simpler approaches. Large, mission or life critical projects were recommended to use more rigor and validation.

Since the development of these approaches, there have been many more models created to help determine where and when to employ agile approaches. Boehm and Turner adopted some of the elements from DSDM and Crystal to develop a popular assessment model to help determine if projects should be undertaken with agile or more traditional approaches.

Based on these previous models and expanded to consider the middle ground of hybrid approaches, the following model is proposed. It represents a synthesis of several suitability filter attributes to help organizations assess and discuss whether projects should be undertaken using predictive, hybrid, or agile approaches.

X3.2 OVERVIEW OF THE MODEL

Organizational and project attributes are assessed under three main categories:

◆ **Culture.** Is there a supportive environment with buy-in for the approach and trust in the team?

◆ **Team.** Is the team of a suitable size to be successful in adopting agile, do its members have the necessary experience and access to business representatives to be successful?

◆ **Project.** Are there high rates of change? Is incremental delivery possible? How critical is the project?

Questions in each of these categories are answered and the results plotted on a radar chart. Clusters of values around the center of the chart indicate a good fit for agile approaches. Results around the outside indicate a predictive approach may be more suitable. Values in the middle portion (between agile and predictive) indicate a hybrid approach could work well. An example is shown in Figure X3-1.

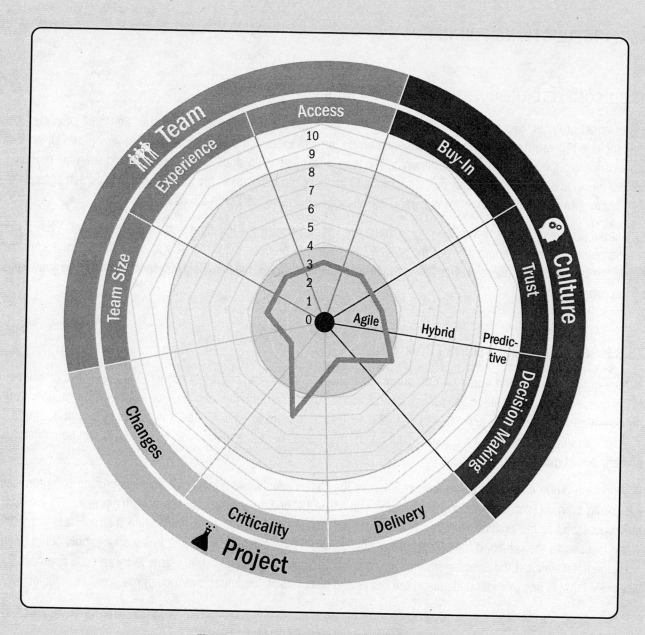

Figure X3-1. Model for Suitability of Agile Approach

X3.3 INSTRUCTIONS FOR USE

X3.3.1 COMPLETE THE QUESTIONNAIRE AS A GROUP

For small projects, this group may simply be the sponsor, technical lead, and a customer. For large projects, this may include representatives from the sponsoring group, project execution team, impacted business group(s), project governance group(s), and customer community. The idea is that just as no single stakeholder should estimate or plan a project because of representing only one viewpoint and having personal bias; so too should no single person assess the suitability of an approach since any one person will also have a limited view with a bias.

Instead, the value of the tool is the conversation it encourages with the invested parties of the project. Even if the results point to a hybrid approach, but the stakeholders want to proceed with a largely agile or predictive approach, follow the stakeholder consensus. This tool is a high-level diagnostic only, the final decision should rest and be supported by the people involved.

X3.3.2 SCORE THE QUESTIONS FROM 1 TO 10

As a group, discuss and agree (or compromise) on a score that most accurately reflects the subjective evaluation of the question. While definitive options are only provided for the start, middle, and end points of the answer spectrum representing scores of 1, 5, and 10, it is fine (and desirable) to use scores such as 2 for "almost a 1, but not quite," or 7 for "somewhere between a 5 and a 10." Again, the assessment is a discussion tool—views will be subjective and shades of gray are to be expected.

When the group cannot agree on a score, discuss the issues openly and honestly. Before suggesting compromises (i.e., using average scores or marking PMO scores with a blue "X" and the development team with a green "O"), consider how successful is the project likely to be when the participants cannot agree on completing a simple assessment? When discussing the issues, if the differences of opinion can be identified—then great, it is working; now come to an agreement. Likewise, if the assessment indicates a predictive approach but everyone wants to try an agile approach (or vice versa) that is fine too, just understand the issues and discuss how the impacts of the approach will be handled.

X3.3.3 INTERPRET THE RESULTS

Mark the answers from the questions on a blank suitability assessment chart and connect the points. Results clustered around the center in the agile zone indicate a good fit for a purely agile approach.

Results predominantly in the hybrid zone indicate some combination of agile and predictive approaches might work best. However, it is also possible that an agile approach with some additional risk reduction steps such as extra education and training or extra validation and documentation rigor in the case of high criticality projects may suffice. Alternatively, a predictive approach with some proof-of-concept work or extra processes could also work.

Results predominantly in the predictive zone indicate a good fit for a purely predictive approach. As mentioned in Section X3.3.2 (Score the Questions step), this diagnostic tool is aimed at starting meaningful conversations with the impacted parties about the most appropriate approach to use. If the approach suggested by the tool is not acceptable it is allowed to use a different approach. Use the results as inputs to the risk management process, since the tool indicates mismatches that will need to be managed.

X3.4 SUITABILITY FILTER QUESTIONS

X3.4.1 CATEGORY: CULTURE

X3.4.1.1 BUY-IN TO APPROACH

Is there senior sponsor understanding and support for using an agile approach for this project? See Figure X3-2.

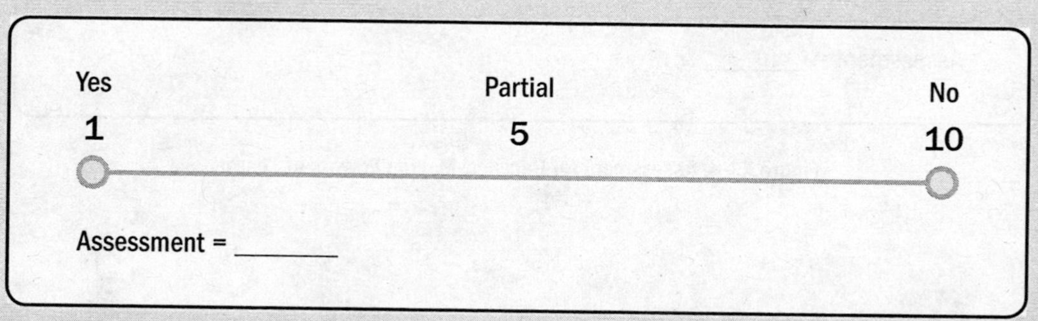

Yes	Partial	No
1	5	10

Assessment = _____

Figure X3-2. Buy-In to Approach Assessment

X3.4.1.2 TRUST IN TEAM

Considering the sponsors and the business representatives who will be working with the team. Do these stakeholders have confidence that the team can transform their vision and needs into a successful product or service—with ongoing support and feedback going both directions? See Figure X3-3.

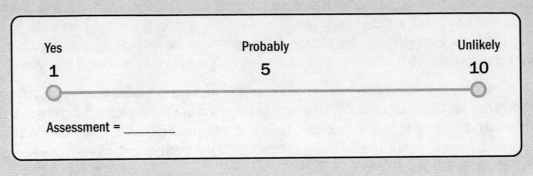

Figure X3-3. Trust in Team Assessment

X3.4.1.3 DECISION-MAKING POWERS OF TEAM

Will the team be given autonomy to make their own local decisions about how to undertake work? See Figure X3-4.

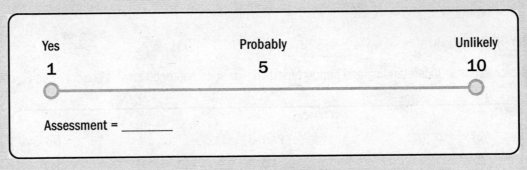

Figure X3-4. Assessment for Decision-Making Powers of Team

X3.4.2 CATEGORY: TEAM

X3.4.2.1 TEAM SIZE

What is the size of the core team? Use this scale: 1-9 = 1, 10-20 = 2, 21-30 = 3, 31-45 = 4, 46-60 = 5, 61-80 = 6, 81-110 = 7, 111-150 = 8, 151 – 200 = 9, 201+ = 10. See Figure X3-5.

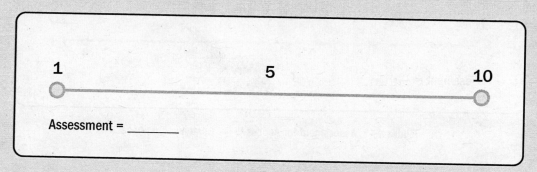

Figure X3-5. Team Size Assessment

X3.4.2.2 EXPERIENCE LEVELS

Considering the experience and skill levels of the core team roles. While it is normal to have a mix of experienced and inexperienced people in roles, for agile projects to go smoothly; it is easier when each role has at least one experienced member. See Figure X3-6.

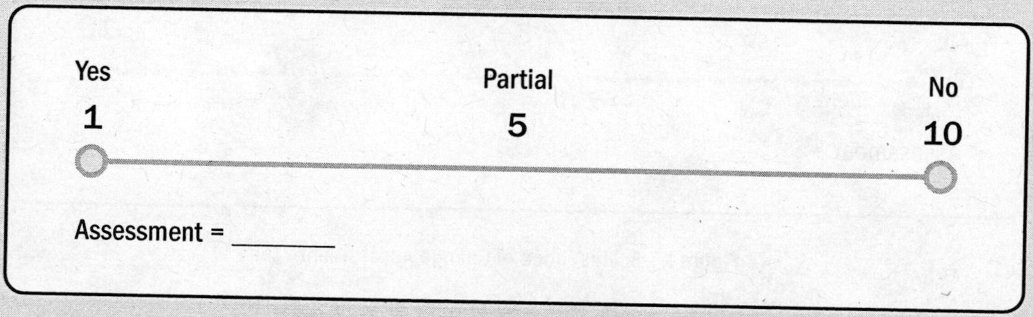

Figure X3-6. Experience Level Assessment

X3.4.2.3 ACCESS TO THE CUSTOMER/BUSINESS

Will the team have daily access to at least one business/customer representative to ask questions and get feedback? See Figure X3-7.

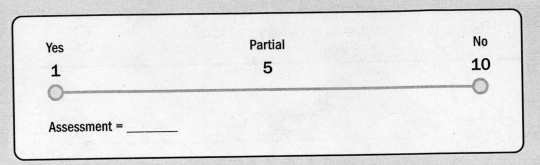

Figure X3-7. Assessment for Access to the Customer/Business

X3.4.3 CATEGORY: PROJECT

X3.4.3.1 LIKELIHOOD OF CHANGE

What percentage of requirements are likely to change or be discovered on a monthly basis? See Figure X3-8.

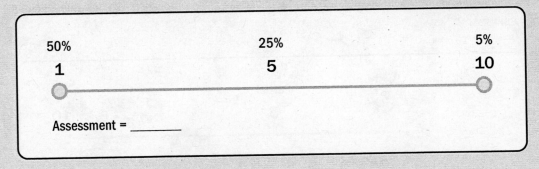

Figure X3-8. Likelihood of Change Assessment

X3.4.3.2 CRITICALITY OF PRODUCT OR SERVICE

To help determine likely levels of additional verification and documentation rigor that may be required, assess the criticality of the product or service being built. Using an assessment that considers loss due to possible impact of defects, determine what a failure could result in. See Figure X3-9.

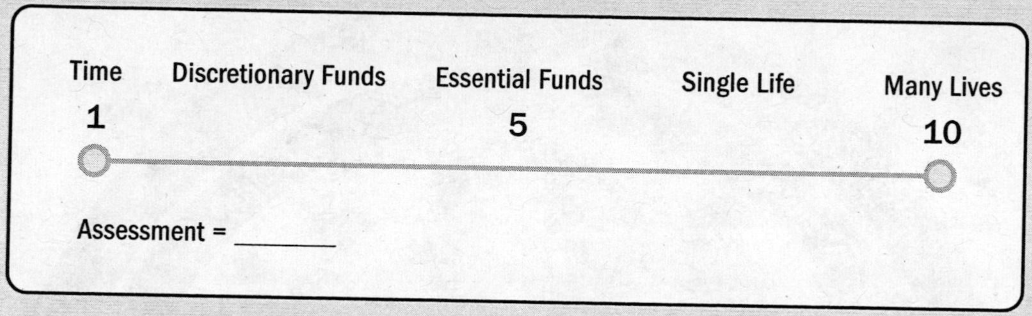

Figure X3-9. Assessment for Criticality of Product or Service

X3.4.3.3 INCREMENTAL DELIVERY

Can the product or service be built and evaluated in portions? Also, will business or customer representatives be available to provide timely feedback on increments delivered? See Figure X3-10.

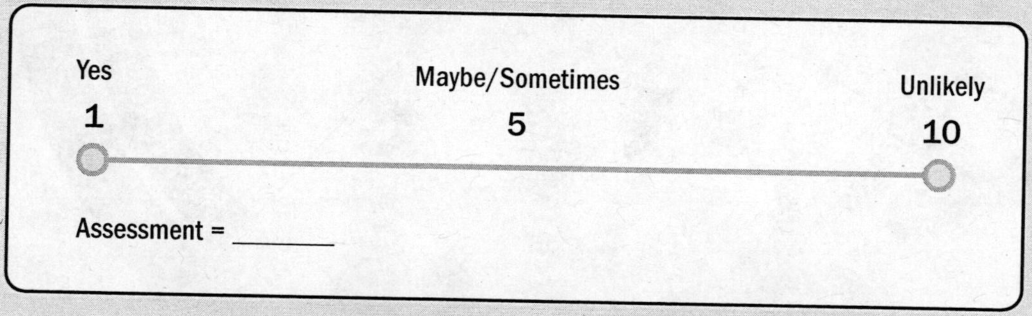

Figure X3-10. Incremental Delivery Assessment

X3.5 SUITABILITY ASSESSMENT CHART

Figure X3-11 is the radar chart used for the suitability assessment.

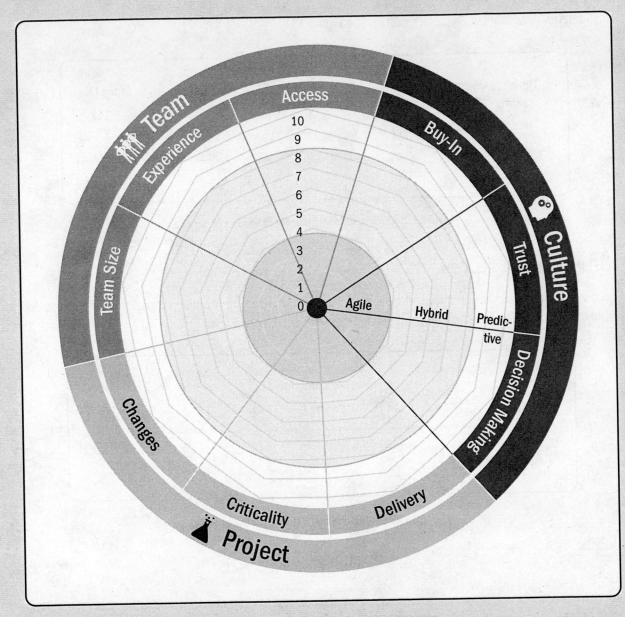

Figure X3-11. Suitability Assessment Radar Chart

X3.5.1 CASE STUDIES

To illustrate how the radar chart works, here are two examples of using the model to score very different types of projects. The first is an example of an online drug store project (see Figure X3-12) and the second (Figure X3-13) is an example of a military messaging system. These two case studies illustrate some of the variances seen on projects. Central clustering indicates a good fit for agile approaches, peripheral scores indicate predictive approaches might be more suitable. Some projects are centered around the middle but then spike out on one or two axes. These projects may be best solved with a hybrid approach.

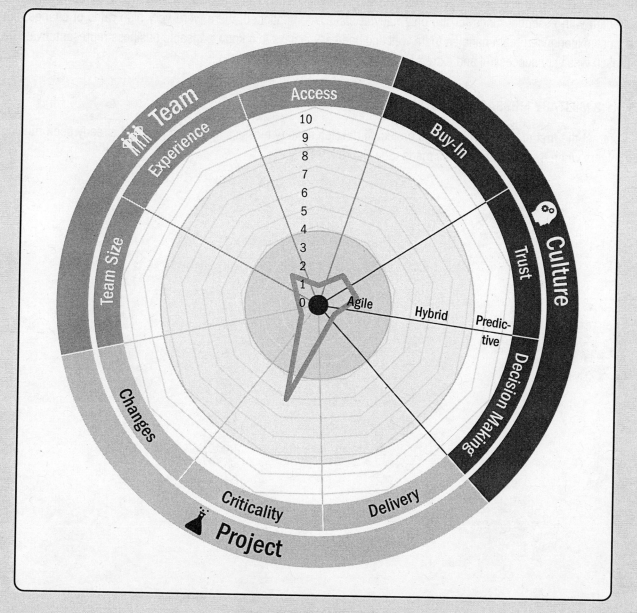

Figure X3-12. Drug Store Project

X3.5.1.1 DRUG STORE EXAMPLE

The project was to develop an online drug store to sell cheaper Canadian prescription drugs to (primarily) U.S. customers. The sale of these drugs is a contentious subject in Canada as well as the U.S. and as a result the industry is characterized by swift regulation changes and fierce competition. The project faced extremely volatile requirements with major changes week on week. It used very short (2-day) iterations and weekly releases to tackle the high rates of change.

As shown in Figure X3-12, high levels of buy-in and trust are evident for those who worked in an empowered way. The visual nature of the website made it easy to show new increments of functionality, but the system criticality was fairly high with essential funds for the pharmacy at stake. As mentioned, there were very high rates of change, but the small experienced team handled them well and had easy access to a knowledgeable business representative. The approach was very successful and extremely agile.

X3.5.1.2 MILITARY MESSAGING SYSTEM EXAMPLE

Contrast the first example with a large project to develop military messaging system that had already been running for 5 years when the assessment was made. See Figure X3-13.

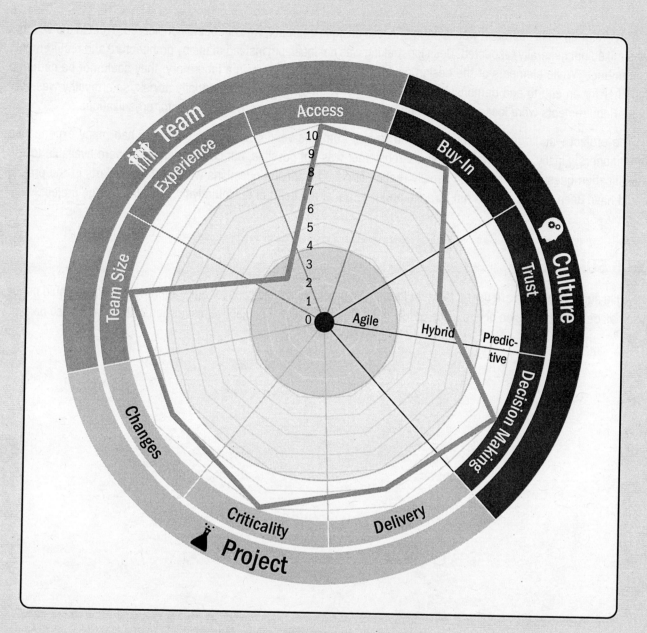

Figure X3-13. Military Messaging Example

Buy-in for an agile approach was lacking because an agile approach was not being considered. Trust in the vendors was mixed but generally respected. Decision making was not local, but instead made by architecture and requirements committees. While elements of the design could be tested incrementally in a laboratory, they could not be gathered together for an end to end demonstration of functionality. Many lives were potentially at risk, so criticality was very high. Requirements were locked down because changes impacted so many subcontractor organizations.

The project was large with more than 300 people from one vendor alone, but each role had many experienced practitioners. Finally, access to the business/customer was not possible, but contract analysts were available to ask specification questions to and they usually replied or asked clarifying questions within 10 days. Parts of the project could have been carved off and run as agile projects, but at the heart of the initiative was a single large project.

X3.6 SUMMARY

Agile suitability filters are useful tools for identifying potential fits and gaps for agile approaches. They should not be used as definitive inclusion or exclusion gates, but instead as topics for objective discussion with all interested parties.

REFERENCES

[1]   *Manifesto for Agile Software Development.* (2001). Retrieved from http://agilemanifesto.org/

[2]   Project Management Institute. 2013. *Managing Change in Organizations: A Practice Guide.* Newtown Square, PA: Author.

[3]   Project Management Institute. 2017. *A Guide to the Project Management Body of Knowledge (PMBOK® Guide) –* Sixth Edition. Newtown Square, PA: Author.

[4]   Project Management Institute. 2013. *Software Extension to the PMBOK® Guide Fifth Edition.* Newtown Square, PA: Author.

BIBLIOGRAPHY

The following are suggested additional reading materials, subdivided by section and/or topic:

SECTION 2—AN INTRODUCTION TO AGILE

Briggs, Sara. "Agile Based Learning: What Is It and How Can It Change Education?" *Opencolleges.edu.au* February 22, 2014, retrieved from http://www.opencolleges.edu.au/informed/features/agile-based-learning-what-is-it-and-how-can-it-change-education/.

Manifesto for Agile Software Development, 2001, http://agilemanifesto.org/.

Peha, Steve. "Agile Schools: How Technology Saves Education (Just Not the Way We Thought it Would)." InfoQ. June 28, 2011, retrieved from https://www.infoq.com/articles/agile-schools-education.

Principles behind the Agile Manifesto, 2001, http://agilemanifesto.org/principles.html.

Rothman, Johanna. 2007. *Manage It! Your Guide to Modern, Pragmatic Project Management.* Raleigh: Pragmatic Bookshelf.

Sidky, Ahmed (Keynote). 2015. https://www.slideshare.net/AgileNZ/ahmed-sidky-keynote-agilenz.

Stacey Complexity Model. 2016. http://www.scrum-tips.com/2016/02/17/stacey-complexity-model/.

SECTION 3—LIFE CYCLE SELECTION

"Agile Modeling (AM) Home Page: Effective Practices for Modeling and Documentation," *Agile Modeling*, (n.d.), http://www.agilemodeling.com/

Anderson, David, and Andy Carmichael. 2016. *Essential Kanban Condensed.* Seattle: Blue Hole Press.

Anderson, David. 2010. *Kanban: Successful Evolutionary Change for Your Technology Business.* Seattle: Blue Hole Press.

Benson, Jim, and Tonianne DeMaria Barry. 2011. *Personal Kanban: Mapping Work | Navigating Life*. Seattle: Modus Cooperandi Press.

Burrows, Mike. 2014. *Kanban from the Inside: Understand the Kanban Method, connect it to what you already know, introduce it with impact*. Seattle: Blue Hole Press.

Domain Driven Design Community. 2016. http://dddcommunity.org/.

Gothelf, Jeff, and Josh Seiden. 2016. *Lean UX: Designing Great Products with Agile Teams*. Sebastopol: O'Reilly Media.

Hammarberg, Marcus, and Joakim Sunden. 2014. *Kanban in Action*. Shelter Island: Manning Publications.

"Kanban," *Wikipedia*, last modified May 4, 2017, retrieved on November 22, 2016 from https://en.wikipedia.org/wiki/Kanban.

"Kanban *(development)*," Wikipedia, last modified May 4, 2017, retrieved on November 29, 2016 from https://en.wikipedia.org/wiki/Kanban_(development).

Larsen, Diana, and Ainsley Nies. 2016. *Liftoff: Start and Sustain Successful Agile Teams*. Raleigh: Pragmatic Bookshelf.

"Learning Kanban," *Leankit*, (n.d.), https://leankit.com/learn/learning-kanban/.

Leopold, Klaus, and Siegrfried Kaltenecker. 2015. *Kanban Change Leadership: Creating a Culture of Continuous Improvement*. Hoboken: Wiley.

"Make a big impact with software products and projects!" *Impact Mapping*, (n.d.), https://www.impactmapping.org/.

Patton, Jeff, and Peter Economy. 2014. *User Story Mapping: Discover the Whole Story, Build the Right Product*. Sebastopol: O'Reilly Media.

Reinertsen, Donald. 2009. *The Principles of Product Development Flow: Second Generation Lean Product Development*. Redondo Beach: Celeritas Publishing.

Rothman, Johanna. "Dispersed vs. Distributed Teams," *Rothman Consulting Group*, Inc., October 25, 2010, http://www.jrothman.com/mpd/2010/10/dispersed-vs-distributed-teams/.

Schwaber, Ken, and Jeff Sutherland. "The Scrum Guide™," *Scrum.org*, July 2016, http://www.scrumguides.org/scrum-guide.html and http://www.scrumguides.org/docs/scrumguide/v2016/2016-Scrum-Guide-US.pdf#zoom=100.

Skarin, Mattias. 2015. *Real-World Kanban: Do Less, Accomplish More with Lean Thinking*. Raleigh: Pragmatic Bookshelf.

"The High Cost of Multitasking: 40% of Productivity Lost by Task Switching," *Wrike.com*, September 24, 2015, https://www.wrike.com/blog/high-cost-of-multitasking-for-productivity/.

Wells, Don. "Extreme Programming: A Gentle Introduction," *Extreme Programming*, October 8, 2013, http://www.extremeprogramming.org/.

SECTION 4—IMPLEMENTING AGILE:

Amabile, Teresa, and Steven Kramer. 2011. *The Progress Principle: Using Small Wins to Ignite Joy, Engagement, and Creativity at Work.* Boston: Harvard Business Review Press.

"Early Warning Signs of Project Trouble—Cheat Sheet, 2017, https://agilevideos.com/wp-content/uploads/2017/02/WarningSignsOfProjectTrouble-CheatSheet.pdf.

Dweck, Carol. 2006. *Mindset: The New Psychology of Success.* New York: Penguin Random House.

Kaner, Sam. *Facilitator's Guide to Participatory Decision-Making.* 3rd ed. 2014. San Francisco: Jossey-Bass.

Keith, Kent. *The Case for Servant Leadership.* 2008. Westfield: Greenleaf Center for Servant Leadership.

Rothman, Johanna. 2016. *Agile and Lean Program Management: Scaling Collaboration Across the Organization.* Victoria, British Columbia: Practical Ink.

Rothman, Johanna. "Dispersed vs. Distributed Teams," *Rothman Consulting Group,* Inc., October 25, 2010, http://www.jrothman.com/mpd/2010/10/dispersed-vs-distributed-teams/.

Rothman, Johanna. 2007. *Manage It! Your Guide to Modern, Pragmatic Project Management.* Raleigh: Pragmatic Bookshelf.

Rothman, Johanna. 2016. *Manage Your Project Portfolio: Increase Your Capacity and Finish More Projects.* Raleigh: Pragmatic Bookshelf.

Schwaber, Ken, and Jeff Sutherland. "The Scrum Guide™," *Scrum.org,* July 2016, http://www.scrumguides.org/scrum-guide.html and http://www.scrumguides.org/docs/scrumguide/v2016/2016-Scrum-Guide-US.pdf#zoom=100.

Sinek, Simon. 2011. *Start with Why: How Great Leaders Inspire Everyone to Take Action.* New York: Portfolio, Penguin Random House.

"The High Cost of Multitasking: 40% of Productivity Lost by Task Switching," *Wrike.com,* September 24, 2015, https://www.wrike.com/blog/high-cost-of-multitasking-for-productivity/.

EXPERIENCE REPORTS:

"Experience Reports," *Agile Alliance,* (n.d.), https://www.agilealliance.org/resources/experience-reports/.

PROJECT AND TEAM HEALTH:

"Early Warning Signs of Project Trouble—Cheat Sheet." 2017. https://agilevideos.com/wp-content/uploads/2017/02/WarningSignsOfProjectTrouble-CheatSheet.pdf

"TeamHealth Radar – Summary View," *Agilehealth.* 2014. http://agilityhealthradar.com/wp-content/uploads/2014/11/bigradar.gif.

RESOURCE EFFICIENCY:

Modig, Niklas, and Pär Åhlström. 2015. *This is Lean: Resolving the Efficiency Paradox*. London: Rheologica Publishing.

Rothman, Johanna. "Resource Efficiency vs. Flow Efficiency, Part 5: How Flow Changes Everything," *Rothman Consulting Group, Inc.*, September 20, 2015, http://www.jrothman.com/mpd/agile/2015/09/resource-efficiency-vs-flow-efficiency-part-5-how-flow-changes-everything/.

SCALING:

Disciplined Agile 2.X—A Process Decision Framework. 2016. http://www.disciplinedagiledelivery.com/.

Kniberg, Henrik. "Scaling Agile @ Spotify with Tribes, Squads, Chapters & Guilds," *Crisp*, November 14, 2012, http://blog.crisp.se/2012/11/14/henrikkniberg/scaling-agile-at-spotify.

"Overview—Large Scale Scrum," *LeSS*. 2016. http://less.works/.

"SAFe® for Lean Software and System Engineering," *SAFe®*. 2016. http://www.scaledagileframework.com/.

SKILLS:

Beck, Kent. *Paint Drip People*, August 4, 2016, https://www.facebook.com/notes/kent-beck/paint-drip-people/1226700000696195/.

"Generalizing Specialists: Improving Your IT Career Skills," *Agile Modeling*, (n.d.), http://www.agilemodeling.com/essays/generalizingSpecialists.htm.

Hunter, Brittany. "Of Software Designers & Broken Combs," *Atomic Object*, June 27, 2013, https://spin.atomicobject.com/2013/06/27/broken-comb-people/.

SECTION 5—IMPLEMENTING AGILE: DELIVERING IN AN AGILE ENVIRONMENT

Larsen, Diana, and Ainsley Nies. 2016. *Liftoff: Start and Sustain Successful Agile Teams*. Raleigh: Pragmatic Bookshelf.

RETROSPECTIVES:

Derby, Esther, and Diana Larsen. 2006. *Agile Retrospectives: Making Good Teams Great*. Raleigh: Pragmatic Bookshelf.

Gonçalves, Luis, and Ben Linders. 2015. *Getting Value out of Agile Retrospectives: A Toolbox of Retrospective Exercises*. Victoria, British Columbia: Leanpub.

BACKLOG:

Adzic, Gojko, Marjory Bissett, and Tom Poppendieck. 2012. *Impact Mapping: Making a Big Impact with Software Products and Projects.* Woking, Surrey: Provoking Thoughts.

Patton, Jeff, and Peter Economy. 2014. *User Story Mapping: Discover the Whole Story, Build the Right Product.* Sebastopol: O'Reilly Media.

Rothman, Johanna. "We Need Planning; Do We Need Estimation?" *Rothman Consulting Group, Inc.*, January 21, 2015, http://www.jrothman.com/mpd/project-management/2015/01/we-need-planning-do-we-need-estimation/.

STANDUPS:

Brodzinski, Pawel. "Effective Standups around Kanban Board," *Brodzinski.com*, December 30, 2011, http://brodzinski.com/2011/12/effective-standups.html.

Fowler, Martin. "It's Not Just Standing Up: Patterns for Daily Standup Meetings," *Martinfowler.com*, February 21, 2016, http://martinfowler.com/articles/itsNotJustStandingUp.html.

Hefley, Chris. "How to Run Effective Standups and Retrospectives," *Leankit*, September 15, 2014, https://leankit.com/blog/2014/09/run-effective-standups-retrospectives/.

EARNED VALUE:

Griffiths, Mike. "A Better S Curve and Simplified EVM," *Leading Answers*, June 6, 2008, http://leadinganswers.typepad.com/leading_answers/2008/06/a-better-s-curve-and-simplified-evm.html.

SECTION 6—ORGANIZATIONAL CONSIDERATIONS FOR AGILE PROJECTS

Bankston, Arlen, and Sanjiv Augustine. *Agile Team Performance Management: Realizing the Human Potential of Teams*, June 14, 2010, www.lithespeed.com/transfer/Agile-Performance-Management.pptx.

Browder, Justin, and Brian Schoeff. *Perfect Strangers: How Project Managers and Developers Relate and Succeed.* CreateSpace Independent Publishing Platform, 2016, https://www.createspace.com/.

Griffiths, Mike. "Agile Talent Management," *Leading Answers*, October 14, 2015, http://leadinganswers.typepad.com/leading_answers/2015/10/agile-talent-management.html.

Kohn, Alfie. 1999. *Punished by Rewards: The Trouble with Gold Stars, Incentive Plans, A's, Praise, and Other Bribes.* New York: Mariner Books.

Mar, Kane. "How to do Agile Performance Reviews," *Scrumology*, (n.d.), https://scrumology.com/how-to-do-agile-performance-reviews/.

McChrystal, Stanley, Tantum Collins, David Silverman, and Chris Fussell. 2015. *Team of Teams: New Rules of Engagement for a Complex World.* New York: Portfolio, Penguin Random House.

Pink, Daniel. 2011. *Drive: The Surprising Truth About What Motivates Us.* New York: Riverhead Books.

SECTION 7—A CALL TO ACTION (INSPECTION WITHOUT ADAPTATION IS FUTILE)

Dennis, Pascal. 2006. *Getting the Right Things Done: A Leader's Guide to Planning and Execution.* Cambridge: Lean Enterprise Institute.

Griffiths, Mike. "Introducing Agile Methods: Mistakes to Avoid—Part 3," *Leading Answers*, March 15, 2007, http://leadinganswers.typepad.com/leading_answers/2007/03/introducing_agi_2.html.

Little, Jason. *Lean Change Management: Innovative Practices for Managing Organizational Change.* Happy Melly Express, 2014, http://www.happymelly.com/category/hm-express/.

Rising, Linda, and Mary Lynne Manns. 2004. *Fearless Change: Patterns for Introducing New Ideas.* Upper Saddle River: Addison-Wesley Professional.

"The IDEAL Model," *Software Engineering Institute, Carnegie Mellon,* 2006, http://www.sei.cmu.edu/library/assets/idealmodel.pdf.

ANNEX A1—*PMBOK® GUIDE* MAPPING

Larsen, Diana and Ainsley Nies. 2016. *Liftoff: Start and Sustain Successful Agile Teams.* Raleigh: Pragmatic Bookshelf.

ANNEX A2—AGILE MANIFESTO MAPPING

Manifesto for Agile Software Development, 2001, http://agilemanifesto.org/.

Principles behind the Agile Manifesto, 2001, http://agilemanifesto.org/principles.html.

ANNEX A3—OVERVIEW OF AGILE AND LEAN FRAMEWORKS

Agile Business Consortium, 2014, https://www.agilebusiness.org/what-is-dsdm.

Ambler, Scott. "The Agile Unified Process," *Ambysoft,* May 13, 2006, http://www.ambysoft.com/unifiedprocess/agileUP.html.

Anderson, David. 2010. *Kanban: Successful Evolutionary Change for Your Technology Business.* Seattle: Blue Hole Press.

Beedle, Mike. *Enterprise Scrum: Executive Summary: Business Agility for the 21st Century,* January 7, 2017, http://www.enterprisescrum.com/enterprise-scrum/.

Cockburn, Alistair. 2004. *Crystal Clear: A Human-Powered Methodology for Small Teams.* Upper Saddle River: Pearson Education.

Cockburn, Alistair. "Crystal Methodologies," *alistair.cockburn.us*, March 28, 2014, http://alistair.cockburn.us/Crystal+methodologies.

Disciplined Agile 2.X—A Process Decision Framework, 2016, http://www.disciplinedagiledelivery.com/.

Joint MIT-PMI-INCOSE Community of Practice on Lean in Program Management. 2012. *The Guide to Lean Enablers for Managing Engineering Programs.* Newtown Square, PA: Author.

"Kanban," *Wikipedia*, last modified May 4, 2017, retrieved on November 22, 2016 from https://en.wikipedia.org/wiki/Kanban.

"Kanban *(development)*," *Wikipedia*, last modified May 4, 2017, retrieved on November 29, 2016 from https://en.wikipedia.org/wiki/Kanban_(development).

Reddy, Ajay, and Jack Speranza. 2015. *The Scrumban [R]Evolution: Getting the Most Out of Agile, Scrum, and Lean Kanban.* Boston: Addison-Wesley Professional.

"Overview—Large Scale Scrum," *LeSS*, 2016, http://less.works/.

"SAFe® for Lean Software and System Engineering," *SAFe®*, 2016, http://www.scaledagileframework.com/.

Schwaber, Ken, and Jeff Sutherland. "The Scrum Guide™," *Scrum.org*, July 2016, http://www.scrumguides.org/scrum-guide.html and http://www.scrumguides.org/docs/scrumguide/v2016/2016-Scrum-Guide-US.pdf#zoom=100.

"Scrum of Scrums," *Agile Alliance*, (n.d.), https://www.agilealliance.org/glossary/scrum-of-scrums/.

"Scrumban," Wikipedia, March 2, 2017, https://en.wikipedia.org/wiki/Scrumban.

"State of Agile Report: Agile Trends," *VersionOne*, 2017, http://stateofagile.versionone.com/.

Sutherland Jeff. "Agile Can Scale: Inventing and Reinventing SCRUM in Five Companies." *Cutter IT Journal* 14, no. 12 (2001): 5–11. http://www.controlchaos.com/storage/scrum-articles/Sutherland_200111_proof.pdf.

"The 2015 State of Agile Development," *Scrum Alliance®*, 2015, https://www.forrester.com/report/The+2015+State+Of+Agile+Development/-/E-RES122910

Wells, Don. "Extreme Programming: A Gentle Introduction," *Extreme Programming*, October 8, 2013, http://www.extremeprogramming.org/.

Why Scrum? State of Scrum Report, 2016, https://www.scrumalliance.org/why-scrum/state-of-scrum-report/2016-state-of-scrum.

APPENDIX X2—ATTRIBUTES THAT INFLUENCE TAILORING

Griffiths, Mike. "Agile Suitability Filters," *Leading Answers*, 2007, http://leadinganswers.typepad.com/leading_answers/files/agile_suitability_filters.pdf.

Jeffries, Ron. "We Tried Baseball and It Didn't Work," *ronjeffries.com*, May 2, 2006, http://ronjeffries.com/xprog/articles/jatbaseball/.

Rothman, Johanna. "One Experimental Possibility: Self-Organization from Component Teams to Feature Teams," *Rothman Consulting Group, Inc.*, September 23, 2014, http://www.jrothman.com/mpd/agile/2014/09/one-experimental-possibility-self-organization-from-component-teams-to-feature-teams/.

GLOSSARY

1. ACRONYMS

ATDD	acceptance test-driven development
BDD	behavior-driven development
BRD	business requirement documents
DA	Disciplined Agile
DoD	definition of done
DoR	definition of ready
DSDM	Dynamic Systems Development Method
Evo	evolutionary value delivery
LeSS	Large-Scale Scrum
LSD	Lean Software Development
PDCA	Plan-Do-Check-Act
PMO	project management office
ROI	return on investment
RUP	rational unified process
SAFe®	Scaled Agile Framework®
SBE	specification by example
XP	eXtreme Programming

2. DEFINITIONS

A3. A way of thinking and a systematic problem-solving process that collects the pertinent information on a single A3-size sheet of paper.

Acceptance Test-Driven Development (ATDD). A method of collaboratively creating acceptance test criteria that are used to create acceptance tests before delivery begins.

Agile. A term used to describe a mindset of values and principles as set forth in the Agile Manifesto.

Agile Coach. An individual with knowledge and experience in agile who can train, mentor, and guide organizations and teams through their transformation.

Agile Life Cycle. An approach that is both iterative and incremental to refine work items and deliver frequently.

Agile Manifesto. The original and official definition of agile values and principles.

Agile Mindset. A way of thinking and behaving underpinned by the four values and twelve principles of the Agile Manifesto.

Agile Practitioner. A person embracing the agile mindset who collaborates with like-minded colleagues in cross-functional teams. Also referred to as agilist.

Agile Principles. The twelve principles of agile project delivery as embodied in the Agile Manifesto.

Agile Unified Process. A simplistic and understandable approach to developing business application software using agile techniques and concepts. It is a simplified version of the Rational Unified Process (RUP).

Agilist. See *Agile Practitioner.*

Anti-Pattern. A known, flawed pattern of work that is not advisable.

Automated Code Quality Analysis. The scripted testing of code base for bugs and vulnerabilities.

Backlog. See *Product Backlog.*

Backlog Refinement. The progressive elaboration of project requirements and/or the ongoing activity in which the team collaboratively reviews, updates, and writes requirements to satisfy the need of the customer request.

Behavior-Driven Development (BDD). A system design and validation practice that uses test-first principles and English-like scripts.

Blended Agile. Two or more agile frameworks, methods, elements, or practices used together such as Scrum practiced in combination with XP and Kanban Method.

Blocker. See *Impediment.*

Broken Comb. Refers to a person with various depths of specialization in multiple skills required by the team. Also known as Paint Drip. See also *T-shaped* and *I-shaped.*

Burndown Chart. A graphical representation of the work remaining versus the time left in a timebox.

Burnup Chart. A graphical representation of the work completed toward the release of a product.

Business Requirement Documents (BRD). Listing of all requirements for a specific project.

Cadence. A rhythm of execution. See also *Timebox*.

Collective Code Ownership. A project acceleration and collaboration technique whereby any team member is authorized to modify any project work product or deliverable, thus emphasizing team-wide ownership and accountability.

Continuous Delivery. The practice of delivering feature increments immediately to customers, often through the use of small batches of work and automation technology.

Continuous Integration. A practice in which each team member's work products are frequently integrated and validated with one another.

Cross-Functional Team. A team that includes practitioners with all the skills necessary to deliver valuable product increments.

Crystal Family of Methodologies. A collection of lightweight agile software development methods focused on adaptability to a particular circumstance.

Daily Scrum. A brief, daily collaboration meeting in which the team reviews progress from the previous day, declares intentions for the current day, and highlights any obstacles encountered or anticipated. Also known as daily standup.

Definition of Done (DoD). A team's checklist of all the criteria required to be met so that a deliverable can be considered ready for customer use.

Definition of Ready (DoR). A team's checklist for a user-centric requirement that has all the information the team needs to be able to begin working on it.

DevOps. A collection of practices for creating a smooth flow of delivery by improving collaboration between development and operations staff.

Disciplined Agile (DA). A process decision framework that enables simplified process decisions around incremental and iterative solution delivery.

Double Loop Learning. A process that challenges underlying values and assumptions in order to better elaborate root causes and devise improved countermeasures rather than focusing only on symptoms.

Dynamic Systems Development Method (DSDM). An agile project delivery framework.

Evolutionary Value Delivery (EVO). Openly credited as the first agile method that contains a specific component no other methods have: the focus on delivering multiple measurable value requirements to stakeholders.

eXtreme Programming. An agile software development method that leads to higher quality software, a greater responsiveness to changing customer requirements, and more frequent releases in shorter cycles.

Feature-Driven Development. A lightweight agile software development method driven from the perspective of features valued by clients.

Fit for Purpose. A product that is suitable for its intended purpose.

Fit for Use. A product that is usable in its current form to achieve its intended purpose.

Flow Master. The coach for a team and service request manager working in a continuous flow or Kanban context. Equivalent to *Scrum Master*.

Framework. A basic system or structure of ideas or facts that support an approach.

Functional Requirement. A specific behavior that a product or service should perform.

Functional Specification. A specific function that a system or application is required to perform. Typically represented in a functional specifications document.

Hoshin Kanri. A strategy or policy deployment method.

Hybrid Approach. A combination of two or more agile and non-agile elements, having a non-agile end result.

IDEAL. An organizational improvement model that is named for the five phases it describes: initiating, diagnosing, establishing, acting, and learning.

Impact Mapping. A strategic planning technique that acts as a roadmap to the organization while building new products.

Impediment. An obstacle that prevents the team from achieving its objectives. Also known as a blocker.

Increment. A functional, tested, and accepted deliverable that is a subset of the overall project outcome.

Incremental Life Cycle. An approach that provides finished deliverables that the customer may be able to use immediately.

Information Radiator. A visible, physical display that provides information to the rest of the organization enabling up-to-the-minute knowledge sharing without having to disturb the team.

I-shaped. Refers to a person with a single deep area of specialization and no interest or skill in the rest of the skills required by the team. See also *T-Shaped* and *Broken Comb*.

Iteration. A timeboxed cycle of development on a product or deliverable in which all of the work that is needed to deliver value is performed.

Iterative Life Cycle. An approach that allows feedback for unfinished work to improve and modify that work.

Kaizen Events. Events aimed at improvement of the system.

Kanban Board. A visualization tool that enables improvements to the flow of work by making bottlenecks and work quantities visible.

Kanban Method. An agile method inspired by the original Kanban inventory control system and used specifically for knowledge work.

Large Scale Scrum (LeSS). Large-Scale Scrum is a product development framework that extends Scrum with scaling guidelines while preserving the original purposes of Scrum.

Lean Software Development (LSD). Lean software development is an adaptation of lean manufacturing principles and practices to the software development domain and is based on a set of principles and practices for achieving quality, speed, and customer alignment.

Life Cycle. The process through which a product is imagined, created, and put into use.

Mobbing. A technique in which multiple team members focus simultaneously and coordinate their contributions on a particular work item.

Organizational Bias. The preferences of an organization on a set of scales characterized by the following core values: exploration versus execution, speed versus stability, quantity versus quality, and flexibility versus predictability.

Organizational Change Management. A comprehensive, cyclic, and structured approach for transitioning individuals, groups, and organizations from the current state to a future state with intended business benefits.

Paint-Drip. See *Broken Comb*.

Pairing. See *Pair Work*.

Pair Programming. Pair work that is focused on programming.

Pair Work. A technique of pairing two team members to work simultaneously on the same work item.

Personas. An archetype user representing a set of similar end users described with their goals, motivations, and representative personal characteristics.

Pivot. A planned course correction designed to test a new hypothesis about the product or strategy.

Plan-Do-Check-Act (PDCA). An iterative management method used in organizations to facilitate the control and continual improvement of processes and products.

Plan-Driven Approach. See *Predictive Approach*.

Predictive Approach. An approach to work management that utilizes a work plan and management of that work plan throughout the life cycle of a project.

Predictive Life Cycle. A more traditional approach, with the bulk of planning occurring up-front, then executing in a single pass; a sequential process.

Project Management Office (PMO). A management structure that standardizes the project-related governance processes and facilitates the sharing of resources, methodologies, tools, and techniques.

Product Backlog. An ordered list of user-centric requirements that a team maintains for a product.

Product Owner. A person responsible for maximizing the value of the product and who is ultimately responsible and accountable for the end product that is built. See also *Service Request Manager*.

Progressive Elaboration. The iterative process of increasing the level of detail in a project management plan as greater amounts of information and more accurate estimates become available.

Refactoring. A product quality technique whereby the design of a product is improved by enhancing its maintainability and other desired attributes without altering its expected behavior.

Retrospective. A regularly occurring workshop in which participants explore their work and results in order to improve both process and product.

Rolling Wave Planning. An iterative planning technique in which the work to be accomplished in the near term is planned in detail, while the work in the future is planned at a higher level.

Scaled Agile Framework (SAFe®). A knowledge base of integrated patterns for enterprise-scale lean–agile development.

Scrum. An agile framework for developing and sustaining complex products, with specific roles, events, and artifacts.

Scrumban. A management framework that emerges when teams employ Scrum as the chosen way of working and use the Kanban Method as a lens through which to view, understand, and continuously improve how they work.

Scrum Board. An information radiator that is utilized to manage the product and sprint backlogs and show the flow of work and its bottlenecks.

Scrum Master. The coach of the development team and process owner in the Scrum framework. Removes obstacles, facilitates productive events and defends the team from disruptions. See also *Flow Master*.

Scrum of Scrums. A technique to operate Scrum at scale for multiple teams working on the same product, coordinating discussions of progress on their interdependencies, and focusing on how to integrate the delivery of software, especially in areas of overlap.

Scrum Team. Describes the combination of development team, scrum master, and process owner used in Scrum.

Self-Organizing Team. A cross-functional team in which people fluidly assume leadership as needed to achieve the team's objectives.

Servant Leadership. The practice of leading through service to the team, by focusing on understanding and addressing the needs and development of team members in order to enable the highest possible team performance.

Service Request Manager. The person responsible for ordering service requests to maximize value in a continuous flow or Kanban environment. Equivalent to product owner.

Siloed Organization. An organization structured in such a way that it only manages to contribute a subset of the aspects required for delivering value to customers. For contrast, see *Value Stream*.

Single Loop Learning. The practice of attempting to solve problems by just using specific predefined methods, without challenging the methods in light of experience.

Smoke Testing. The practice of using a lightweight set of tests to ensure that the most important functions of the system under development work as intended.

Specification by Example (SBE). A collaborative approach to defining requirements and business-oriented functional tests for software products based on capturing and illustrating requirements using realistic examples instead of abstract statements.

Spike. A short time interval within a project, usually of fixed length, during which a team conducts research or prototypes an aspect of a solution to prove its viability.

Sprint. Describes a timeboxed iteration in Scrum.

Sprint Backlog. A list of work items identified by the Scrum team to be completed during the Scrum sprint.

Sprint Planning. A collaborative event in Scrum in which the Scrum team plans the work for the current sprint.

Story Point. A unit-less measure used in relative user story estimation techniques.

Swarming. A technique in which multiple team members focus collectively on resolving a specific impediment.

Technical Debt. The deferred cost of work not done at an earlier point in the product life cycle.

Test-Driven Development. A technique where tests are defined before work is begun, so that work in progress is validated continuously, enabling work with a zero defect mindset.

Timebox. A fixed period of time, for example, 1 week, 1 fortnight, 3 weeks, or 1 month. See also *Iteration*.

T-shaped. Refers to a person with one deep area of specialization and broad ability in the rest of the skills required by the team. See also *I-Shaped* and *Broken Comb*.

User Story. A brief description of deliverable value for a specific user. It is a promise for a conversation to clarify details.

User Story Mapping. A visual practice for organizing work into a useful model to help understand the sets of high-value features to be created over time, identify omissions in the backlog, and effectively plan releases that deliver value to users.

UX Design. The process of enhancing the user experience by focusing on improving the usability and accessibility to be found in the interaction between the user and the product.

Value Stream. An organizational construct that focuses on the flow of value to customers through the delivery of specific products or services.

Value Stream Mapping. A lean enterprise technique used to document, analyze, and improve the flow of information or materials required to produce a product or service for a customer.

INDEX

Agile principles
    agile-based learning and, 2
    cross-functional teams and, 43
    defined, 150
    readiness for change and, 73
Agile roles, 40–41
Agile suitability filters, 25
Agile teams
    attributes of successful, 39–40
    roles in, 40–41
Agile unified process, 150
Agilist. *See* Agile practitioner
Anti-pattern(s)
    defined, 150
    standups and, 55
Approach(es)
    blending of, 31
    term use in guide, 11
ATDD. *See* Acceptance test-driven development
Automated code quality analysis, 150
Automated testing, 31, 56
Automation, 7

B

Backlog. *See* Product backlog
Backlog refinement, 52–53
    conducting meetings for, 53
    defined, 150
    refinement length and, 52
Baselines, 61
Basics, 1–5
    agile-based learning and, 2
    development of guide, 1
    disruptive technologies and, 3
    organization of guide, 5
    reason for guide, 2
    in-scope/out-of-scope items, 4
Batch sizes, 42
BDD. *See* Behavior-driven development
Behavior-driven development (BDD)
    defined, 150
    value delivery and, 56
Big Dig, Boston, 15
Blended agile, 150

Blending of approaches, 31
Blocker. *See* Impediment
Boston Big Dig, 15
Bottlenecks, 35, 42, 64
BRD. *See* Business requirement documents
Broken comb, 150
Budgeting, incremental, 36
Burndown chart
    defined, 150
    feature charts and, 67
    story points and, 62
Burnup chart
    defined, 150
    earned value and, 68–69
    feature charts and, 67
    product backlog, 68
    scope changes and, 64
    story points and, 63
Business practices, 79
Business requirement documents (BRD), 150
Business satisfaction, 60
Business service. *See* Service(s)
Business value delivery, 16, 23, 29

C

Cadence
    defined, 151
    working product delivery and, 57
Call to action, 87
Cancellation option, contracts and, 78
Capacity measures
    iteration-based agile and, 55
    in-the-moment measurements and, 66
    story points and, 66
Change(s). *See also* Uncertainty
    accelerated delivery and, 73
    agile approaches and, 73
    kanban board and, 85
    readiness for, 73–74
    requirements and, 24
    roadblocks to, 74
    safety and, 75
    speed of, agile mindset and, 3
Change control boards, 35

P

Pain points, troubleshooting and, 57–59
Paint-drip. *See* Broken comb
Pairing. *See* Pair work
Pair programming, 102, 153
Pair work, 39
Parking lot, problems and, 54
Part-time assignments, risk and, 45
Pay-as-you-go or pay-what-you-use model, 3
PDCA. *See* Plan-Do-Check-Act
Personas, 153
Personnel, development of, 82
"Phase gates," 77
Pivot, 153
Plan-Do-Check-Act (PDCA), 153
Plan-driven approach, 153
Planning
    feedback and, 29
    iteration-based agile and, 55
    life cycles and, 20
    replanning and, 61
PMBOK Guide, 17, 38
PMO. *See* Project management office
Predictive approaches
    agile approach combined with, 27
    with agile components, 28
    measurements and, 60
Predictive component, agile approach with, 28
Predictive life cycle(s)
    characteristics of, 20–21
    continuum of life cycles and, 19
    defined, 153
Predictive rollout, following agile development, 26–27
Problems
    standups and, 54
    troubleshooting, 57–59
Problem solving, facilitation of, 39–40
Procurement
    business practices and, 79
    contracts and, 77–79
Procurement-heavy organizations, 83
Product, minimum viable, 23

Product backlog. *See also* Backlog refinement
    defined, 153
    initial, ranked for changes, 85
    preparation of, 52
    Scrum framework and, 31
Product backlog burnup chart, 68
Product delivery. *See* Deliveries
Productivity
    boosting, 39–40
    task switching and, 44–45
Product owner
    cross-functional teams and, 38
    defined, 153
    product roadmap and, 52
    role, agile team member, 41
    Scrum framework and, 31
    throughput and, 66
Product roadmap, 52
Progressive elaboration, 153. *See also* Backlog refinement
Progress tracking, 27. *See also* Kanban board
Project(s)
    inherent characteristics and, 18
    large, 15
Project charter, 49–50
Project factors, tailoring options and, 32
Project knowledge, vendors and, 83
Project leaders, stakeholders and, 75
Project life cycles. *See* Life cycle(s)
Project management, goal of, 29
Project Management Institute (PMI®), 1, 43
Project management office (PMO), 81–82
    defined, 153
    demonstrations and, 57
    invitation-oriented, 81
    multidisciplinary, 82
    value-driven, 81
Project manager(s)
    agile environment and
    defined, 38
    role of, 37
    servant leadership and, 38
Project risks, hybrid life cycle and, 29
Project task board
    cumulative flow diagram and, 70
    "walking the," 53
    work in progress and, 25

Team(s). *See also* Agile teams; Cross-functional team(s); Self-organizing team(s)
    accumulating work and, 70
    business practices and, 79
    chartering project and, 49–50
    collocated, 39, 43, 44, 45
    composition of, 38–47
    coordination, multi-team, 80
    core members of, 45
    core writing, guide and, 1
    delivery, 35
    dispersed, 43, 44, 45
    distributed, 43, 46
    facilitator, role of, 41
    self-managing, 39
Team augmentation contracting approach, 76
Team charter, 49–50
Team facilitator, role of, 41
Team leaders, 82
Team members, dedicated, 44–45
Team roles, agile, 40–41
Team structures, 43
Team values, 50
Team workspaces, 46
Technical debt, 154
Technical skills, 36
Technologies, disruptive, 2, 3
Temporary specialists, 45, 83
Test-Driven Development (TDD)
    blending approaches and, 31
    defined, 154
    value delivery and, 56
Testing
    acceptance, 82
    at all levels, 56
    automated, 31, 56
    uncertainty and, 16
Thought processes. *See* Agile mindset
Throughput, 42
    multitasking and, 44
    product owner and, 66
    standups and, 54
Time and materials approach
    graduated, 78
    not-to-exceed, 78

Timebox(es). *See also* Spike(s)
    defined, 154
    standups and, 53
    use of, 12
Tradeoffs, 76
Traffic light status reporting, 60
Training, 82
Transition strategy, hybrid life cycles as, 30
Transparency
    collaboration and, 79
    delivering value and, 87
    success and, 85
Troubleshooting, 57–59, 82
T-shaped, 42, 155

U

Uncertainty. *See also* Change(s)
    complexity and, 7, 13
    exploration of, 16
    medium- to low- degree of, 30
    requirements and, 13, 14, 16, 22, 24
    risk, life cycle selection and, 13–16
    technical degree of, 14
Uncertainty and Complexity Model, 14
Unit testing, 56
Upfront estimation, 27
User Story
    defined, 155
    demonstrations and, 55
    as microdeliverable, 77
User story mapping, 155
U.S. FDA approval process, 26
UX design, 155

V

Value. *See also* Business value delivery; Deliverables
    acceleration of, 30
    contracting techniques and, 77
    delivering, 16, 23, 56
    intermediate, 29
    learning and, 61–62
    metrics and, 60
    optimizing flow of, 38–39